UK price
£6.95

UK price
£6.95

THE CREATIVE BOOK OF

Soft Toys

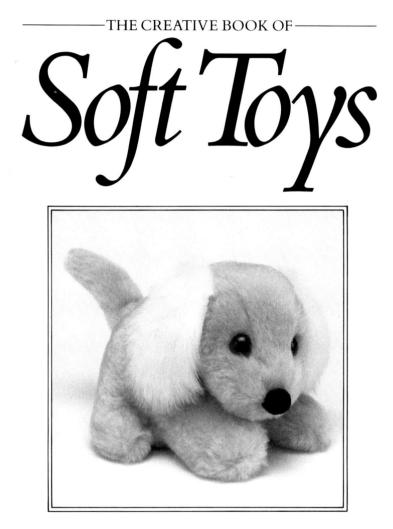

THE CREATIVE BOOK OF

Soft Toys

Sue Quinn

a Salamander book

Published by Salamander Books Limited
LONDON • NEW YORK

Published by Salamander Books Ltd.,
52 Bedford Row,
London WC1R 4LR,
England.

©Salamander Books Ltd. 1987
The copyright on toy designs belongs
exclusively to Sue Quinn
ISBN 0 86101 330 1

Distributed by Hodder and Stoughton Services,
PO Box 6, Mill Road, Dunton Green,
Sevenoaks, Kent TN13 2XX.

All correspondence concerning the content of this volume
should be addressed to Salamander Books Ltd.

CREDITS

Editor-in-chief: Jilly Glassborow

Editor: Ricki Ostrov

Designer: Barry Savage

Photographer: Terry Dilliway

Pattern artwork: Malcolm Porter

Typeset by: The Old Mill, London

Colour separation by: Fotographics Ltd, London – Hong Kong

Printed in Belgium by: Proost International Book Production

CONTENTS

—————— INTRODUCTION ——————

Making soft toys is an enjoyable and rewarding pastime that brings both pleasure and profit to many. The appeal of a soft toy relies largely on the toy's design and character, and within this book Sue Quinn has created a menagerie of charming and beautifully-designed characters that will delight all those that make and play with them. The toys featured range from quick and easy-to-make designs such as the attractive Cheeky Squeeky Mice to more complex creations such as Morris the Monkey and Pan-Pan the Panda — in fact, there is something to suit every taste and sewing ability.

The book opens with an introduction to the equipment, materials and techniques employed in toymaking, essential reading if you are to achieve the best and most professional results. There is information on the equipment needed and its use; the various types of materials available and which to choose; how to prepare the pattern and cut the fabric; plus the numerous techniques referred to throughout the book, such as those required for sewing, turning and stuffing a toy.

Following this are detailed instructions on how to make 25 delightful toys, each design accompanied by a cutting pattern and a series of easy-to-follow step-by-step illustrations.

EQUIPMENT

Before you begin to sew, you must assemble the right equipment. Having the correct tool for the job makes the work easier and ensures that the final result is as attractive as possible.

SCISSORS

One of the most important pieces of equipment is a good sharp pair of scissors. You should actually have at least two pairs; one for cutting out the cardboard used for making the patterns and one for cutting the fabric. A small pair of embroidery scissors with very sharp points are also a must. These are used for piercing the tiny eye holes, for cutting the ear slits and for unpicking thread.

PINS AND NEEDLES

It is very easy to lose pins in the pile of fur fabric, so it is advisable to count the number you use before starting and again when the work is completed. Never leave a pin inside a toy that a child will play with.

Have a wide selection of handsewing needles available. You will soon find the length of needle that suits you best. Have some long darning needles on hand, too, for sewing on the heads of the toys and for embroidering the nose and mouth (see page 17).

BRUSHES

Fur fabrics can quickly lose their fluffiness from all the handling. Brushes are used to bring up the pile and to restore the fabric to its original shape. Teazle brushes are especially good for brushing out fur that has become trapped in the seams. For a large toy, though, a dog brush with similar teeth is much easier to use and covers a larger area. The tiny wire teeth in brushes work loose after a time and become stuck in the fabric, so remove any loose teeth from the brush each time it is used. Also, never use the brush too near to the plastic eyes of the toys, as the surface of the eye can easily become scratched.

SCREWDRIVERS

Screwdrivers are very useful tools for turning the finished toy the right way out. The screwdriver should be a Phillips-type, as the end is blunt enough not to damage the fabric. A knitting needle can also be used, but always use the blunt end.

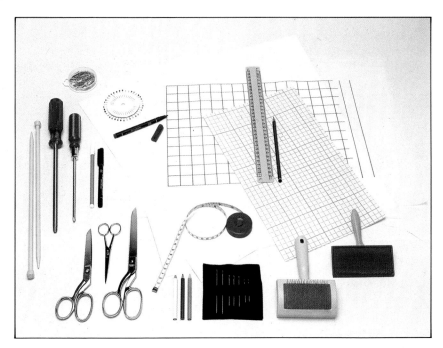

Be sure to use the right tool for each job. Assemble all the equipment before you begin to sew, making sure you have everything you need.

CARDBOARD AND PAPER

Pieces of medium-thickness cardboard are necessary for marking out the pattern pieces. You can buy packages of cardboard in stationery stores, or you can improvise using old cereal packages. Dressmaker's squared paper, used for making the patterns, is available from fabric stores. Alternatively, you can make your own, for which you will need large sheets of thin paper and a ruler and pen to draw up the grid.

PENS AND PENCILS

A quick-drying felt-tip pen is the best type for marking out patterns and for making the cardboard pattern pieces. A soft lead pencil is usually preferred for marking the eye and ear positions, as well as for marking out any other guidelines that must be transferred from the pattern onto the fabric. For dark fabrics, a white chalk pencil is needed to be sure that the outline shows up. There are numerous ones on the market, some of them specifically made for dressmakers.

MATERIALS

There is a wide range of fabrics and threads available for soft toy making, so, when choosing your materials, try to choose the best quality possible. The look and feel of the toy will be improved and the toy will last that much longer.

FUR FABRIC

It is always best to buy high quality fur fabric, if possible. A fur fabric with a woven backing is usually the best, as it has a pleasant, realistic feel. The fabric does not stretch very much, though, and can be difficult to work with. For a beginner, it is best to choose a fur fabric with a knitted backing. These are easily available, do not fray and will stretch slightly, making them easier to work with.

When choosing fur, look at the pile of the material. If too much of the knitted backing can be detected through the fur, it will be disappointing to work with. Feel the knitted side of the fabric. If it is too harsh and hard, again it will be difficult to sew, turn and stuff. A fabric with a supple backing is a much better choice.

FELT

Felt is delightful to work with. It does not fray, it stretches slightly and comes in a wonderful selection of colours. Felt is usually made of man-made fibres; occasionally a pure wool felt is available but these are very expensive. You can buy felt by the metre or yard. Felt is not washable, though, and does not have the strength that other fabrics have. Self-adhesive felts are available but they come in a limited range of colours. Black self-adhesive felt is extremely useful and can be used successfully for the eyes of the toys.

FILLING

There is quite a variety of fillings to choose from, but the general rule is to use the very best. Never use old stockings or tights, or cuttings of fabric. The result will be disappointing and the toy will look lumpy and rather heavy.

Dacron and polyester, which is a man-made fibre, is the best. It is springy, washable, and non-allergic. It is sold in different grades so choose the best you can afford. This filling also comes in different colours, but only buy coloured filling if a dark toy is being made — otherwise the filling will show through.

Fur fabric, felt and thread come in a wide range of colours. Using the best quality you can afford will improve the look of the finished toy.

Kapok is a natural fibre and very fluffy. It is not washable, it is messy to use and not very springy. It does have a beautiful soft feel, though, and could be used for certain types of toys.

Foam chips are not recommended as filling for toys. It is difficult to obtain a good smooth surface to the toy, and tiny particles of foam can be inhaled by small children.

THREAD

A strong sewing thread is the best for the seams. Choose one that contains man-made fibres, as it will stretch and give a little when the toy is being turned and filled. Button thread, or the thickest thread available, is necessary for sewing the heads or limbs in place. The colour range is not as wide as for sewing thread, but this is not too important as most of the stitches should be hidden. Cotton embroidery thread, the non-stranded variety, is very good for embroidering the noses and mouths.

PATTERN PREPARATION

The patterns in this book have all been reduced in size to fit the page. If you look at one of the patterns, you will see that it has been drawn on a grid. Each square on that grid represents 2.5cm (1in). To enlarge the patterns you will need scissors, cardboard, dressmaker's squared paper, a felt-tip pen and a soft lead pencil. The dressmaker's paper must be divided into 2.5cm (1in) squares in order to reproduce the pattern at its full size. If such paper is not readily available, or simply if you wish to save money, you can easily draw up your own grids on some large sheets of thin paper. A long ruler and set square will prove useful for this purpose.

To begin, first lay out a large sheet of the squared paper, flattening it out if it has been folded. Select a starting point on the pattern and look at the square that part of the pattern occupies. Note where the pattern line enters that square and mark the position on one of the larger squares of your grid, making sure you have left lots of space all around. Now examine the same square on the pattern in the book, and note where the line leaves the square. Again, mark that spot on your paper. Next, join the two marks together, noting what happens to the line in between the two points. Follow the line exactly, copying it onto the larger square.

Work around the whole pattern shape in this way, constantly checking and rechecking the general shape of each piece. With a little practice and patience it becomes much easier. Remember, too, to mark the eye positions and slits for the ears, as well as any letters or arrows on the pattern. When you have completed the whole pattern, cut it out very carefully. Now mark around this outline onto pieces of cardboard, copying down all the relevant points. Cut out the cardboard

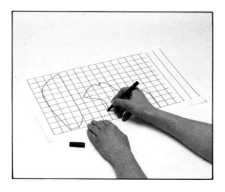

Following the book pattern, draw the full-sized pieces onto the grid.

After drawing the pattern onto cardboard, cut out the pieces.

templates. These will be firm enough to draw around without buckling or tearing, and can be used several times. Keep the paper copy in an envelope in case any of the cardboard pieces are lost.

MARKING AND CUTTING OUT

Lay out the piece of fabric you have selected and check which way the pile goes; mark an arrow on the reverse side of the fabric to remind yourself of the direction of pile. (This is important, as the direction of pile will affect the whole appearance of the toy.)

Lay the cardboard pattern pieces onto the reverse of the fabric, putting the pieces against a fold where indicated. Make sure that the arrows on the pattern pieces point in the same direction as the arrow marked on the fabric. Hold the pattern down with one hand and draw around the shape of the pattern onto the fabric with the other hand. If two asymmetrical fur pieces are required, for instance two body sides, turn the pattern over to get a mirror image for the second piece, but still making sure that the arrow is pointing in the same direction.

Once all the pattern pieces have been marked out, check to make sure that nothing has been omitted. Carefully cut around the outline using your fabric scissors. Where slits or holes are noted, use the small pointed scissors instead.

When using very long fur fabric, for Santa's beard for instance, snip the back carefully without cutting through the actual pile of the fabric so that the fur maintains its length. Felt, velvet and ordinary fabrics can be marked out and cut double thickness; fur fabric should always be marked and cut using a single thickness only.

Outline the pattern pieces onto the fabric using a felt-tip pen.

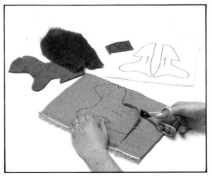

Cut out the material, making sure to use the fabric scissors.

SEWING TECHNIQUES

When sewing a seam, begin by pinning together the two pieces to be joined. Then tack along the seam line, using plain sewing thread and a standard needle. Once the tacking has been completed, take out the pins. Then machine sew along the seam; a 5mm- ($^1/_5$in) seam allowance has been allowed for on the pattern. At the start and end of each seam, reverse stitch twice to ensure that the ends will not open.

A running stitch is used for gathering the raw edges of the head at the neck, for gathering lace or ribbon, and for making noses. Using strong thread and a handsewing needle, sew small straight stitches around the edge of the item to be gathered, then pull the thread gently. Fasten off firmly or the gathering will come loose.

The ladder stitch is used for closing the gap after stuffing the toy.

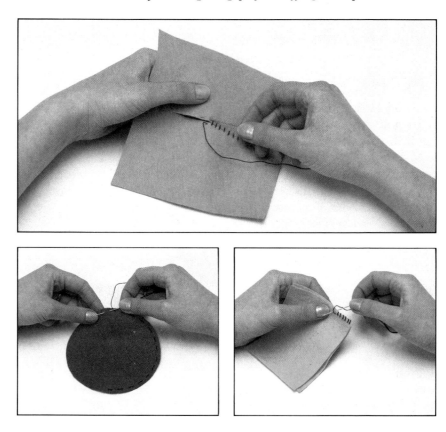

A running stitch is used to gather fabric, lace and ribbon.

Oversewing can be used to join two fabric pieces together.

A ladder stitch is used for closing gaps after the toy has been stuffed and for attaching heads and limbs. When finished, this stitch should be almost invisible. To close a gap, start sewing at the very end and to one side of the gap. Push the needle through from the underside of the fabric so that the knot is underneath. Bring the needle and thread over the gap and make a stitch about 5mm ($^1/_5$in) long on the other side, beginning level with the original stitch and running parallel to the gap. Then take the needle and thread back across the gap and make a stitch on that side. Continue working ladder stitches in this way all the way down the gap, pulling in the raw edges as you go. At the end of the gap, finish off firmly.

To attach the head, begin by holding it firmly onto the body. Then, using strong thread, make a small stitch in the body where the head meets the neck. Next make a small stitch in the head, keeping the entrance hole for the needle level with the exit hole on the body. Continue in this way all around the head and neck, keeping the holes aligned. Sew around the head once or twice and finish off firmly. The same method is used for attaching the arms and legs to the body.

Oversewing is sometimes used to join together the raw edges of two pieces of fabric. Place the two pieces to be joined with the edges level. Starting at one end, push needle and thread through both layers of fabric. Bring the needle through to the other side, then bring the thread over the top of the fabric edges. Insert the needle through the same side of the fabric as the first stitch, about 5mm ($^1/_5$in) away, keeping it level with the first hole. Take needle and thread through the other side. Continue making stitches in this way, bringing needle and thread over the fabric edge each time.

TURNING, STUFFING AND FINISHING

When the toy is sewn up completely, it is time to turn it the right way out. First inspect all seams carefully to make sure there are no holes. Start turning with the ends of the legs and arms, pushing the tips in with the fingers and thumbs, and using a blunt instrument to help where necessary. Turn the body through the gap, easing out a bit at a time.

Once the eyes are inserted, you can procede to stuff the animal. Fluff out the filling between the fingers to be sure there are no lumps. Push small amounts of filling into the ends of the legs and arms, working slowly. Stuff the body cavity, making sure the legs are not wobbly where they meet the body. Push a little more filling into that space if

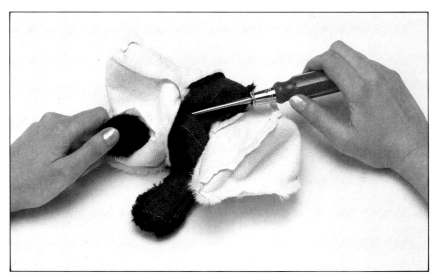

After sewing is completed, start turning the toy at the arms or legs. Use a blunt instrument such as a Phillips screwdriver to help.

necessary. Heads and bodies can be moulded into shape with filling. Only when you are completely satisfied with the shape should the gap be closed. Once the stuffing is completed, brush the seams with care, pulling out any trapped fibres from the stitches.

EYES AND NOSES

There are several different types of eyes available. The best are safety eyes which come with metal or plastic washers. Fixed in the correct manner they are impossible to remove. The stalk of the eye should be pushed through the tiniest of holes in the fabric. The washer should be pushed onto the stalk on the reverse of the fabric as far as it will go. If a fabric has a loose weave or knitted backing it will be necessary to reinforce or strengthen the fabric when using safety eyes. Stick small circles of felt to the back of the material over the holes, or sew around the hole to prevent stretching. An embroidered eye is the best type to use if the toy is for a young child. Round felt eyes can also look effective and should be sewn into place with tiny stitches.

Plastic noses can be purchased and fixed into place using the same method as for safety eyes. Black pom poms can also look good, as can balls made from circles of felt gathered with a running stitch. A number of the noses in this book have been embroidered.

Sewing the Nose and Mouth

To begin, insert the needle and the embroidery thread through the toy from the base of the head to a point approximately 7mm (^{1}/$_4$in) to the left of the nose tip. Be sure to keep the seam in the centre. Pull the needle and thread all the way through the fabric.

Pull the thread over to the other side of the centre seam. Insert the needle through the fabric so that it exits through the seam line approximately 4mm (^{1}/$_6$in) down from the first stitch.

Pull the needle through the fabric and loop the thread through the top straight stitch. Pull it down into a V-shape. Push the needle through the head at a point below the V, still on the seam line. It should reappear to the right of the seam line and down a little.

Take the needle back up to the base of the Y. Insert it through the fabric and bring it out of the fabric at a point on the left side.

Take the needle back up to the centre again and push it through so that it makes an exit underneath the head. This way the thread can be fastened off without being seen.

MATERIALS

Small piece of pastel fur fabric
Small scrap of cotton fabric in
*   contrasting colour*
Small scraps of black and
*   white felt*
Length of white cord
1 squeeker
Filling

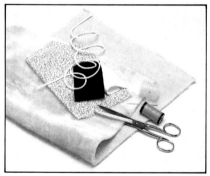

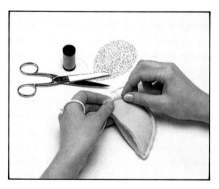

Tack and sew the side body pieces together, leaving the straight edge open. Catch the white cord in the seam, about 15mm (¾in) from the bottom at the position marked on the pattern. Put a knot in the end of the cord to finish off the tail.

With right sides together, tack and sew the cotton base piece to the body, leaving a small gap at the side for turning and filling.

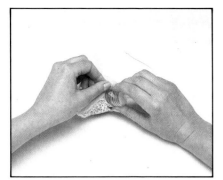

Turn the mouse the right way out. Place a small amount of filling inside, easing it into the nose and one side of the mouse. Push the squeeker into the mouse in a central position. Pack a little more filling around the squeeker so that it is padded on all sides. Neatly ladder stitch the opening.

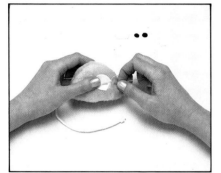

Position the white felt ears onto the head. Firmly oversew to the body along the straight edge. Stitch the black felt eyes to the head below the ears. Pass the threaded needle through from one eye to the other, gently pulling it until you are completely satisfied with the mouse's expression.

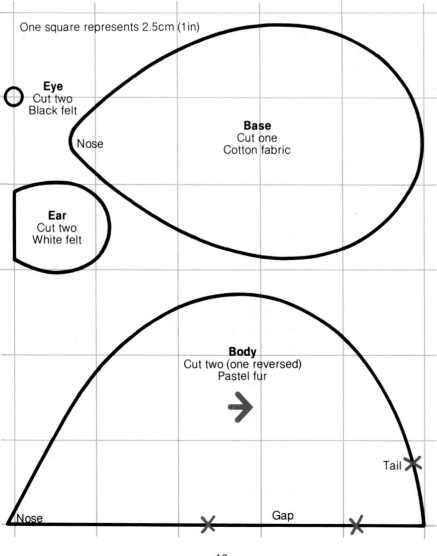

One square represents 2.5cm (1in)

Eye
Cut two
Black felt

Base
Cut one
Cotton fabric

Nose

Ear
Cut two
White felt

Body
Cut two (one reversed)
Pastel fur

Tail

Nose

Gap

MATERIALS

Small piece of lemon fur fabric
Small piece of white fur fabric
Scrap of black felt
Scrap of orange felt
1 jingle bell about 5cm (2in)
*   in diameter*
Ribbon
Filling

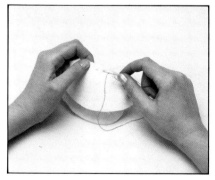

With right sides together, sew the top of the two side body pieces around the head and back along seam A-B. Then sew the under body to the bottom of the side body, starting at point A, matching point B and then back to point A. Cut a small slit in the tummy where indicated and turn the chick the right way out, carefully poking out the tail.

Fill the chick with stuffing, starting with the head. Place a little filling in the body, spreading it evenly along one side. Push the jingle bell inside the body and continue to add stuffing until the bell is well padded on all sides.

Close the gap with a ladder stitch.
Place the wings in position at the
neck and oversew along the straight
edge to hold them in place. Sew the
eye circles in position on the side of
the head with a couple of tiny
stitches. Place the beak centrally
under the eyes and oversew at either
side in the corners. Finally, tie a
ribbon around the chick's neck,
forming a bow.

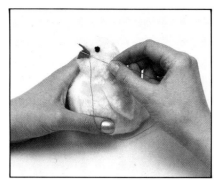

One square represents 2.5cm (1in)

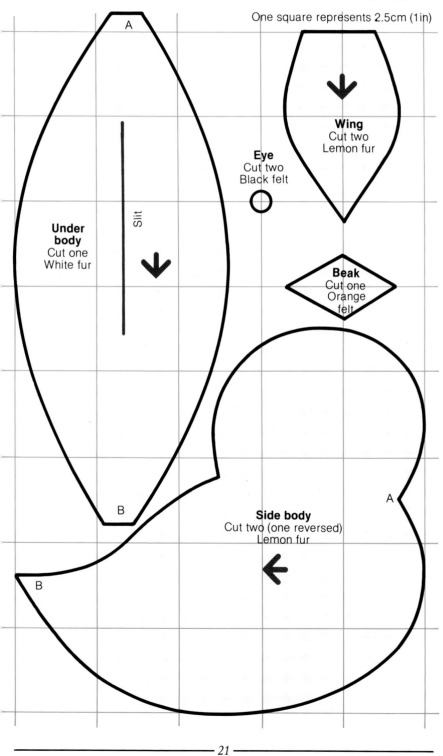

A

Wing
Cut two
Lemon fur

Eye
Cut two
Black felt

Slit

**Under
body**
Cut one
White fur

Beak
Cut one
Orange
felt

B

A

Side body
Cut two (one reversed)
Lemon fur

B

MATERIALS

20cm (8in) lemon fur fabric
Small piece white fur fabric
1 pair safety eyes with washers
35cm (14in) red and white
   striped jersey fabric
3 white pom poms, about 35mm
   (1 ½ in) in width
Filling

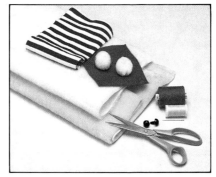

Cut out all the pieces except for the feet. Pierce the fabric at the eye positions. Then tack and sew each section of orange beak to the top gusset pieces between points A and B. Place the two sections right sides together. Tack and sew from C to A, then around the orange beak to point B, then from points B to D.

With right sides together, tack and sew the top and bottom gusset pieces together between points E and F.

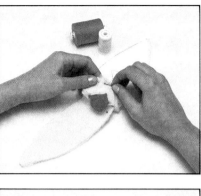

Sew the completed body gusset to the side body, starting at H. Make sure seam E-F on gusset matches that point on body. Finish up at G. Repeat for other side. Tack and sew from J to H. Turn the duck the right way out, pushing out the beak and tail.

Insert safety eyes through the holes made earlier, securing them on the reverse side with washers. Stuff the toy carefully, starting with the beak and head. When nicely rounded, fill the body in the same way. Ladder stitch the back opening and fasten off firmly.

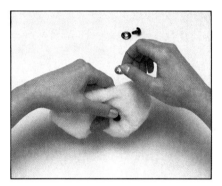

With right sides together, sew the linings onto the wing pieces, leaving the straight edge K-L open for turning. Turn the wings the right side out, poking out the tips. Oversew the tops of the wings and ladder stitch to the side of the body at the neck, with the points of the wings facing toward the back.

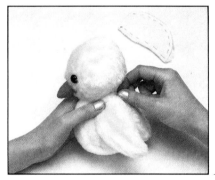

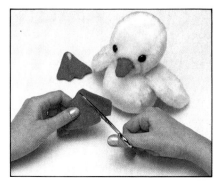

Mark out the foot pattern twice onto two layers of orange felt. Stitch carefully around this outline. Trim away the felt close to the stitches. Make a small slit at the base of each foot and place a tiny amount of filling inside. Oversew the slits, then ladder stitch the feet to the body at the points marked on the body pattern.

For the scarf and hat, cut two rectangles of jersey, one 35cm x 7cm (14in x 3in) for the scarf and the other 15cm x 30cm (6in x 12in) for the hat. Fold both lengthwise, then tack and sew down the long edge. Turn both pieces the right way out. For the scarf, gather the ends of the tube with a running stitch and attach pom poms to each end.

For the hat, take one end of the tube and push it inside itself so that the two raw edges meet around the top. Gather with a running stitch through both layers. Pull tight and finish off firmly. Turn the right way out. Attach a pom pom to the top, fold over slightly and ladder stitch into place on the side of the hat. Turn up the brim at the bottom.

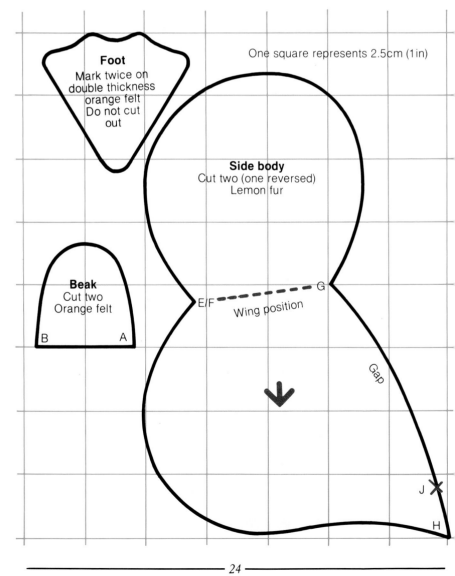

One square represents 2.5cm (1in)

Foot
Mark twice on double thickness orange felt
Do not cut out

Side body
Cut two (one reversed)
Lemon fur

Beak
Cut two
Orange felt

B   A

E/F ‑ ‑ ‑ ‑ ‑ ‑ ‑ G
Wing position

Gap

J

H

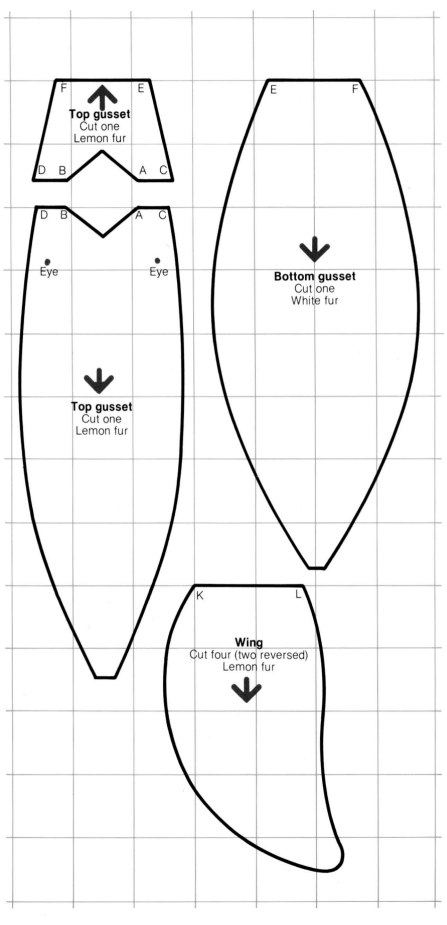

MATERIALS

25cm (10in) gold fur fabric
Small piece of white fur fabric
Scraps of green and orange felt
1 pair 16.5mm brown safety
  eyes with washers
Filling
Black embroidery thread
14cm x 60cm (5½in x 24in) strip
  of gingham
Narrow elastic

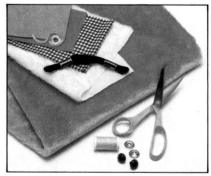

Pierce the fabric carefully at the eye positions and cut along the slit line on head pieces. Tack and sew the gold and white ear pieces together, leaving the straight edges A-B open. Turn the ears, pushing out the points. Oversew edges A-B at the base.

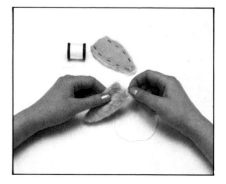

Tack and sew the side head pieces together from C to D, leaving the straight edge open. Push the ear into the head and, with the white ear lining pointing forward towards the nose, ease the raw edge of the ear into the slit. Firmly sew all the layers together. Repeat with the other side.

Turn the head, pushing out the nose tip. Push the safety eyes through the holes made earlier and secure with metal washers. Stuff the head, moulding it into a round shape. Pay particular attention to the bunny's cheeks to give the toy a good expression.

Make a running stitch around raw edge of the neck and pull tight. Oversew several times and secure. Using black embroidery thread, stitch the nose referring to the instructions on page 17.

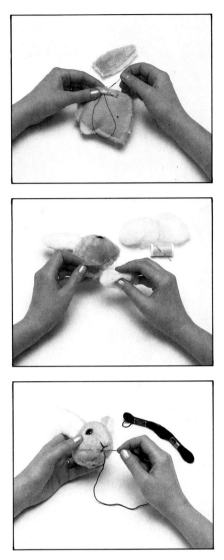

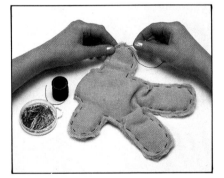

Sew up the darts on either side of the back body. Place the front and back body pieces right sides together. Tack and sew all around, leaving the straight edge open at the top for turning. Turn the body the right way out. Starting with the legs, fill and mould the toy into a semi-sitting position. Sew a running stitch to gather the top raw edge, then finish off securely.

Ladder stitch the head to the body several times. Gather the edge of the round tail piece with a running stitch. Place a small amount of filling in centre, then pull the stitching tight. Finish off tightly, then ladder stitch the tail to the bottom of the bunny's back.

Cut felt for the carrot. Fold the triangular piece lengthwise and sew along the straight edge. Tack and sew the circular piece to the top. Snip a small slit across the top and turn the carrot. Stuff and oversew the slit. Gather the centre of the green leaf and oversew it several times to the top of the carrot. Ladder stitch the carrot to the bunny's arm.

For the skirt, tack and sew the short edges of gingham together. Hem the bottom of the skirt. Turn over the top of the skirt on the wrong side 5mm (¼in) and then 15mm (¾in). Machine sew this casing, leaving a gap of 15mm (¾in) at the back of the skirt. Thread narrow elastic through the gap and adjust to fit the bunny's waist.

One square represents 2.5cm (1in)

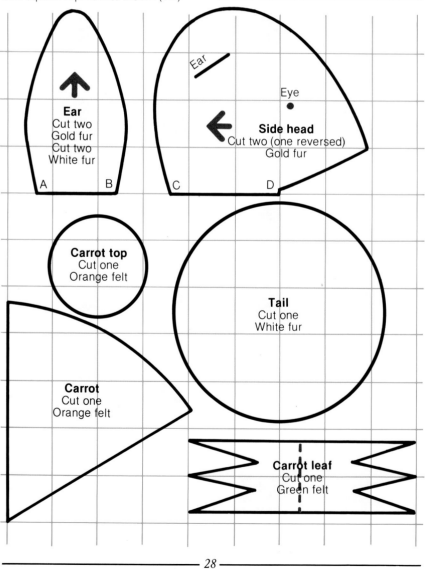

Ear
Cut two
Gold fur
Cut two
White fur

A B C D

Ear

Eye

Side head
Cut two (one reversed)
Gold fur

Carrot top
Cut one
Orange felt

Tail
Cut one
White fur

Carrot
Cut one
Orange felt

Carrot leaf
Cut one
Green felt

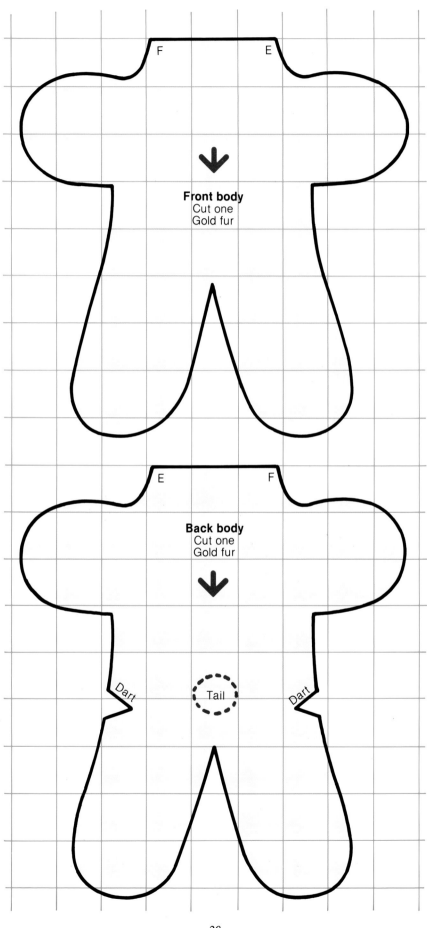

F
E

Front body
Cut one
Gold fur

E
F

Back body
Cut one
Gold fur

Dart
Tail
Dart

MATERIALS

Red/brown fur fabric
Red/brown long fur fabric for
   tail
Small piece of white fur fabric
Scrap of brown felt for ears
1 pair 13.5mm brown safety
   eyes with metal washers
Black embroidery thread
Filling

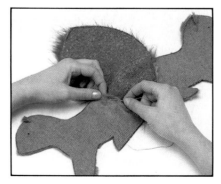

On both the side body pieces, sew up the head dart. Then sew up the dart on the tail. Join the tail to the side body pieces by sewing seam A-B on both sides.

With right sides together, join the two side body pieces by sewing seam C-D, making sure that you match point B, from the nose to the tip of the tail.

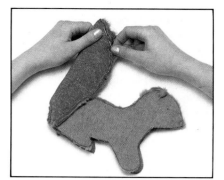

Place the two body gussets right sides together and sew seam E-F, leaving a gap for turning. Join the body gusset to the side body pieces all the way around the body profile. Start at point E through points A and F, then sew back to point E. Finally, sew seam C-E.

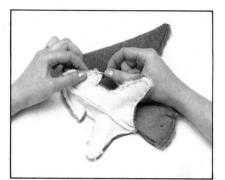

Pierce tiny holes for the eyes at the positions indicated. Starting at the tail tip, turn the squirrel the right way out using a long, blunt tool. Be careful to ease out the ends of the legs. Insert the safety eyes in the holes made earlier and secure on the reverse of the head with the washers.

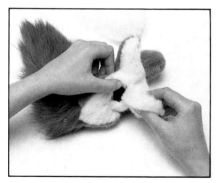

Fill the squirrel with stuffing, placing a small amount in the tail to reach only part of the way up. Add more at the tail base and at the rear of the body. Fill the head, ensuring that the neck is firm. Then fill the legs, using only a small amount of stuffing, making sure they are not too firm.

Finally, stuff the shoulders and tummy of the squirrel, shaping them gently. When satisfied with the general shape of the squirrel, close the gap underneath the body using a ladder stitch.

Cut the ears out of the brown felt. Fold one ear piece in half and oversew it at the base to the side of the head. Make sure that the ear stands upright. Repeat for other ear.

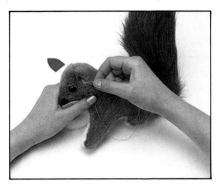

With black embroidery thread, stitch a small nose on the squirrel, referring to the instructions on page 17. If desired, the head can be tilted back and held in place with a few small stitches to give a different expression.

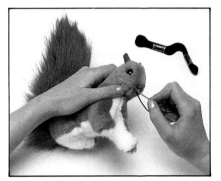

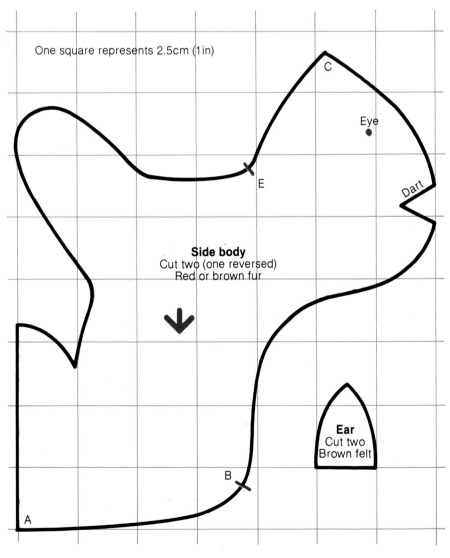

One square represents 2.5cm (1in)

C

Eye

E

Dart

Side body
Cut two (one reversed)
Red or brown fur

Ear
Cut two
Brown felt

B

A

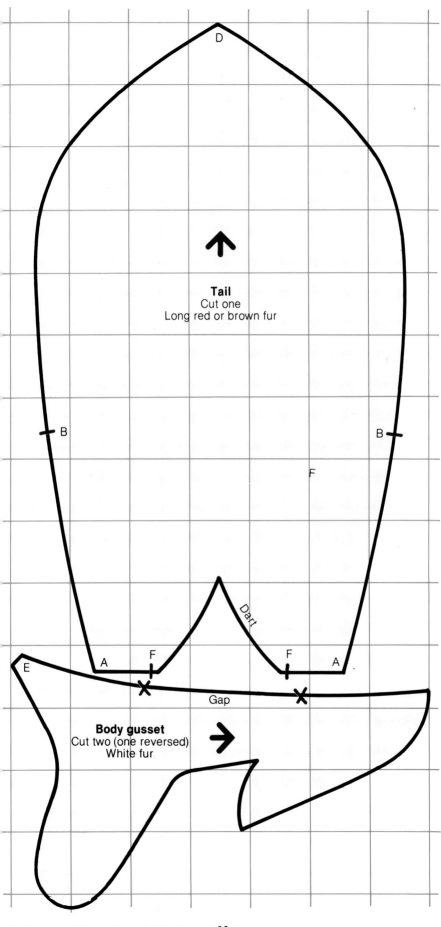

D

Tail
Cut one
Long red or brown fur

B ⊢   ⊣ B

F

Dart

A   F   F   A

E

Gap

Body gusset
Cut two (one reversed)
White fur

MATERIALS

20cm (8in) pink fur fabric
Scraps of pink felt
1 pair 13.5mm safety eyes with
    metal washers
Pink embroidery thread
Narrow elastic
Filling

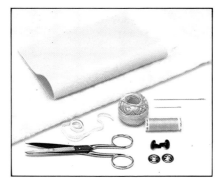

Pierce tiny holes for the eyes and slits for the ears on each side head piece. Close the darts. Sew the ear linings to the ear pieces, leaving the straight edges open. Then turn the ears and fold lengthwise, with felt innermost. With the lining facing forward, push the ears into the slits and sew them in place through all the layers of fabric.

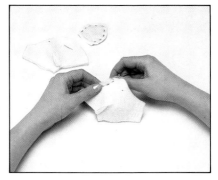

Join the head gusset to the side head, sewing seam G-H. Repeat on the other side. Sew seam J-K under the chin. Open out the nose and, stretching the raw edges to fit, sew in the pink felt circle. Turn the head the right way out.

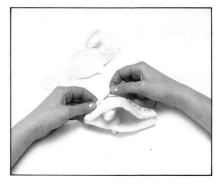

Join the two underbody pieces together by sewing seam A-B, leaving a gap where indicated for turning and filling.

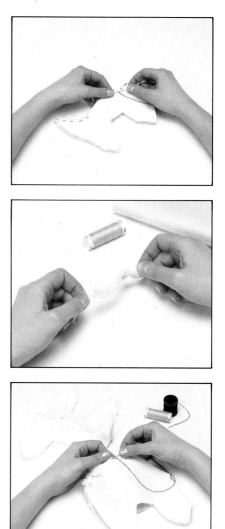

Fold the tail in half lengthwise and sew along the long edge. Insert a piece of elastic slightly longer than the tail through the tube. Oversew at the end, holding the elastic in position. Pull the elastic a little to make the tail curl, and sew into place. Cut off the excess elastic.

On both of the side body pieces, close the darts at the rear. Join the two halves together along seam L-B, catching in the tail at the same time at the rear. Join the underbody to the side body on both sides, starting with seam A-C. Then sew seam D-E, and finally seam F-B.

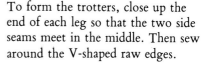

To form the trotters, close up the end of each leg so that the two side seams meet in the middle. Then sew around the V-shaped raw edges.

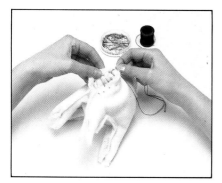

Push the head inside the body so that the right sides are together and the raw edges meet at the neck. Turn the head slightly to one side so that the seam at K is tilted to meet the point marked on the pattern. Sew around the raw edge, joining the head to the body.

Turn the pig the right way out, carefully picking out the points on the trotters. Insert safety eyes in the holes made earlier and secure with metal washers. Stuff the pig, starting at the nose. When the head is completed, start on the feet, adding a little filling at a time.

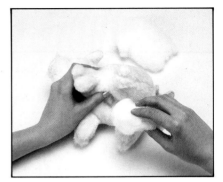

When satisfied with the general shape of the body, close the gap using a ladder stitch. To finish, embroider two pink dots on the end of the snout.

One square represents 2.5cm (1in)

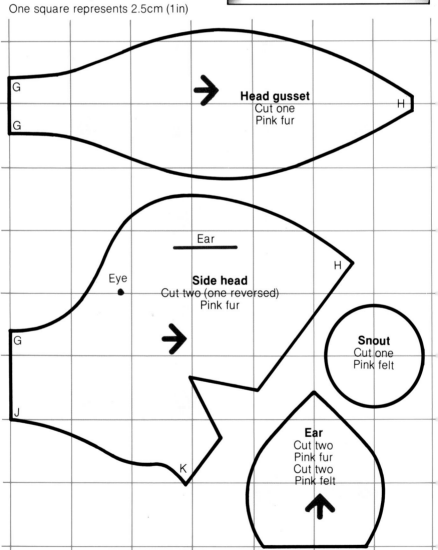

G

G

→ **Head gusset**
Cut one
Pink fur

H

Ear

H

Eye
•

Side head
Cut two (one reversed)
Pink fur

G

→

Snout
Cut one
Pink felt

J

K

Ear
Cut two
Pink fur
Cut two
Pink felt

↑

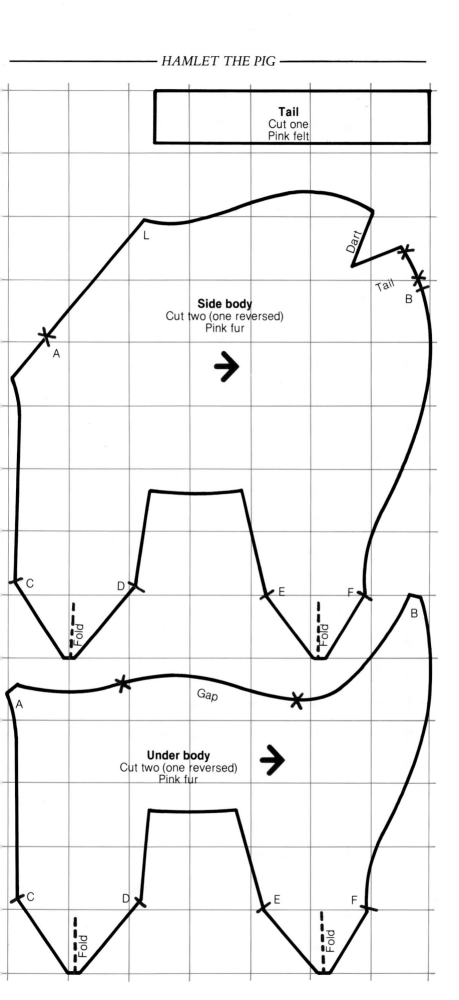

Tail
Cut one
Pink felt

Side body
Cut two (one reversed)
Pink fur

Under body
Cut two (one reversed)
Pink fur

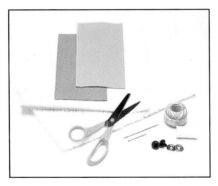

MATERIALS

25cm (10in) fleecy white fur
   fabric
Scraps of velvet or felt for ear
   lining
Scraps of green and yellow felt
1 pair 16.5mm brown
   safety eyes with metal
   washers
Pink embroidery thread
Filling

Sew the ears to the ear linings,
leaving the straight edge open. Turn
ears the right way out; fold in half
lengthwise and oversew the raw
edge. Insert an ear into the slit on
the side of the head, with the lining
facing toward nose. Sew into
position, through all layers of fabric.
Repeat on the other side head piece.

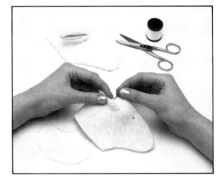

Sew up the dart on each side head
piece. Take the head gusset and sew
to the left hand side of the head,
between A and B. Repeat on the
other side, sewing from B to A, then
continuing to sew the side heads
together from A down to the base of
the neck. Sew the seam under the
chin to the base of the neck.

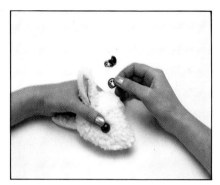

Pierce tiny holes at the eye positions and turn the head the right way out. Insert the safety eyes, securing on the reverse of the fabric with metal washers. Stuff the head firmly and close the gap with a running stitch.

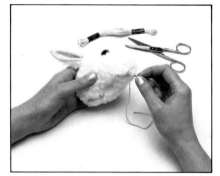

Using pink embroidery thread, embroider a nose and mouth on the lamb, referring to the instructions on page 17.

Fold the green felt grass in half one way and then the other. Sew the folded pieces of grass to the side of the head at the position of the mouth, pulling them tightly into place. Sew the yellow flower to the end of one of the blades of grass. Place the head to one side.

Fold the tail in half lengthwise, right sides together, and sew, leaving the straight edge open. Turn the right way out. On each side body, sew up the dart at the rear. Sew the sides together between E and F. Sew the back seam G-H, inserting the tail at the same time in a downward position at the point marked on the pattern.

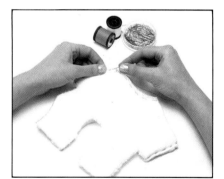

With right sides together, join the two inside body pieces by sewing between points C and D.

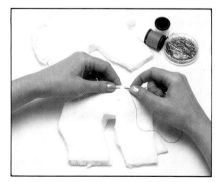

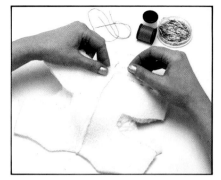

Join the inside body to the side bodies, starting at point O. Work up the leg, across the chest and down the other leg. Repeat at the back of the body, from point N. Sew seam J-K between the legs on both sides. Sew in the foot pads at the base of the legs, easing the raw edge open to fit.

Turn the body the right way out and stuff gently, starting at the bottom of the legs. Once the body is completely filled, gather the raw edge of the neck using a running stitch, and pull tight. Position the head on the body, tilting it slightly to one side; ladder stitch the head and body firmly together.

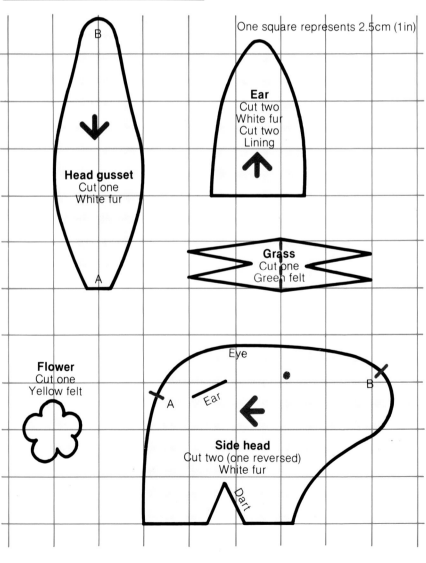

One square represents 2.5cm (1in)

B

Head gusset
Cut one
White fur

A

Ear
Cut two
White fur
Cut two
Lining

Grass
Cut one
Green felt

Flower
Cut one
Yellow felt

Eye

A Ear

B

Side head
Cut two (one reversed)
White fur

Dart

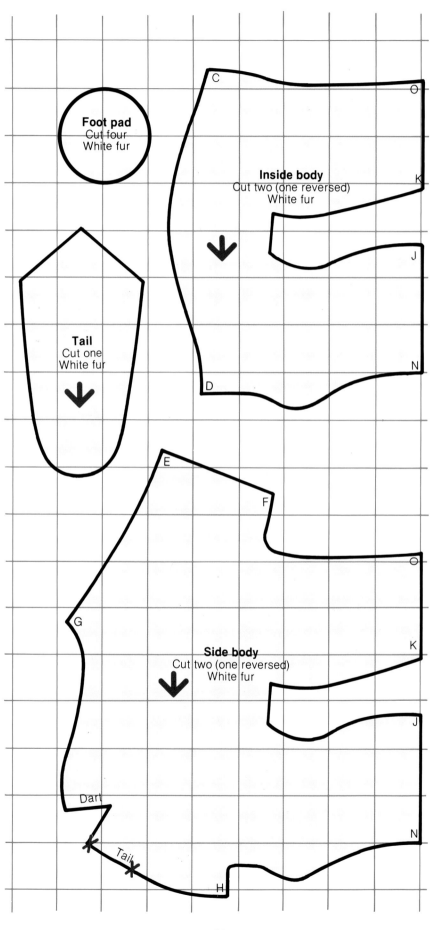

Foot pad
Cut four
White fur

Inside body
Cut two (one reversed)
White fur

C
O
K
J
N
D

Tail
Cut one
White fur

E
F
G
O
K
Side body
Cut two (one reversed)
White fur
J
Dart
Tail
N
H

MATERIALS

30cm (12in) beige fur fabric
Small scrap of white fur fabric
Small scrap of long white fur
Small scrap of black felt
Small scrap of white felt
1 pair 18mm brown safety
   eyes with metal washers
Black embroidery thread
Filling

Sew the ears together, leaving the straight edge open. Turn the ears the right way out, fold lengthwise with the white lining innermost and oversew fold into place. Take the side head pieces and cut slits for the ears and pierce tiny holes for the eyes. Push the raw edges of the ears through the slits and sew into position, with the lining facing forward.

Sew the top head piece to the front head piece between A and B. Then sew the back head piece to the top head piece from C to D. Sew the front, top, and back head to the side head from point E to F. Repeat on other side. Sew the chin piece to the side head from G to H on both sides.

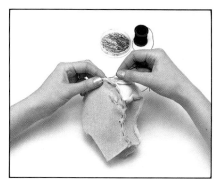

Stitch the white fur nose piece to the head, gently easing the fabric to fit. Turn the head the right way out and insert the safety eyes. Secure the eyes with the metal washers. Stuff the head, adding a little extra filling in the cheeks. Using a running stitch, gather the raw edge of the neck and fasten off securely.

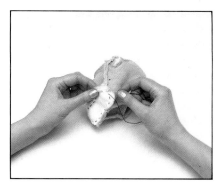

Trim a little fur away from the nose and sew the black nostrils into place. Using black embroidery thread, stitch a straight line for the mouth in a central position just under the cow's nose.

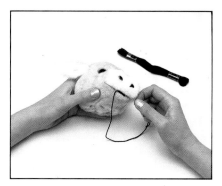

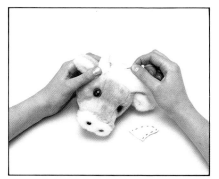

Mark out the horns onto double thickness white felt. Sew around the horn shape, leaving the straight edge open, then cut around the outline using sharp scissors. Turn the horns the right way out and stuff. Stitch around the base, pull tight and fasten off. Ladder stitch the horns into position at either side of the tuft.

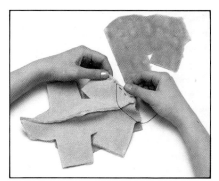

With right sides together, sew the two inside gusset pieces together from J to K. Join the inside gusset to the side body by sewing seam N-O on either side.

Open out the front legs on the body piece. With the right sides together, sew the hoof pieces to the front legs along the straight edge.

Fold the front legs over again along the seam and sew edges Q-P-T to the tip of the hoof. Then open out the back legs and attach the hooves in the same way. Fold the back legs over again and sew edges K-R-T.

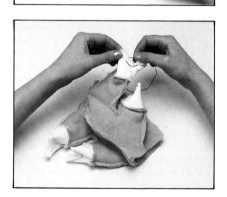

Fold each of the legs so that the seam meets in the centre. Then sew all around the edges of the hooves.

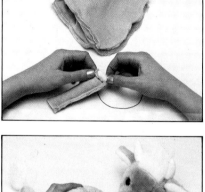

Fold the tail lengthwise and sew along the long edge. Fold the tuft with the *wrong* sides together and sew, then trim close to the stitching. Push the tail end into the tail with the raw edges meeting. Sew across the top of the tail and turn right way out. Sew the back seam of the cow from L to K, catching in the tail at the same time.

Stuff the body, starting with the legs. When satisfied with the overall shape, gather the raw edge at the neck using a running stitch and fasten off securely. Place the head on the body, adjusting the position to suit. Ladder stitch the head firmly into place several times around with strong thread.

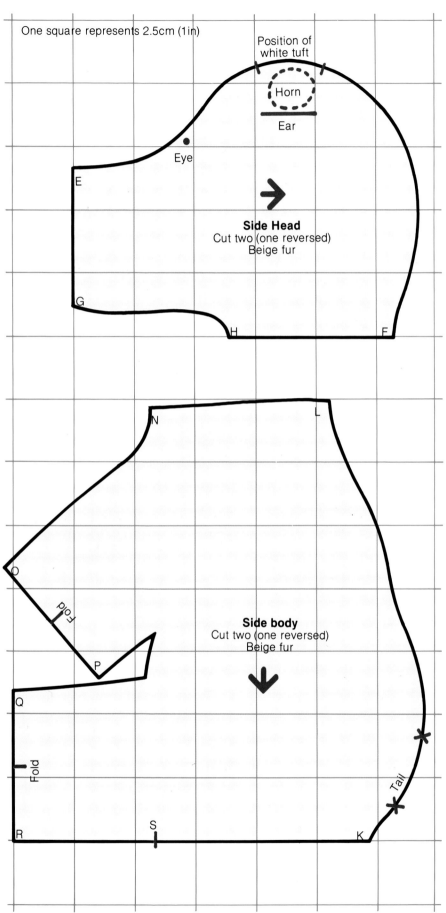

One square represents 2.5cm (1in)

Position of white tuft

Horn

Ear

Eye

Side Head
Cut two (one reversed)
Beige fur

E

G H F

N L

O

Fold

P

Q

Fold

Side body
Cut two (one reversed)
Beige fur

Tail

R S K

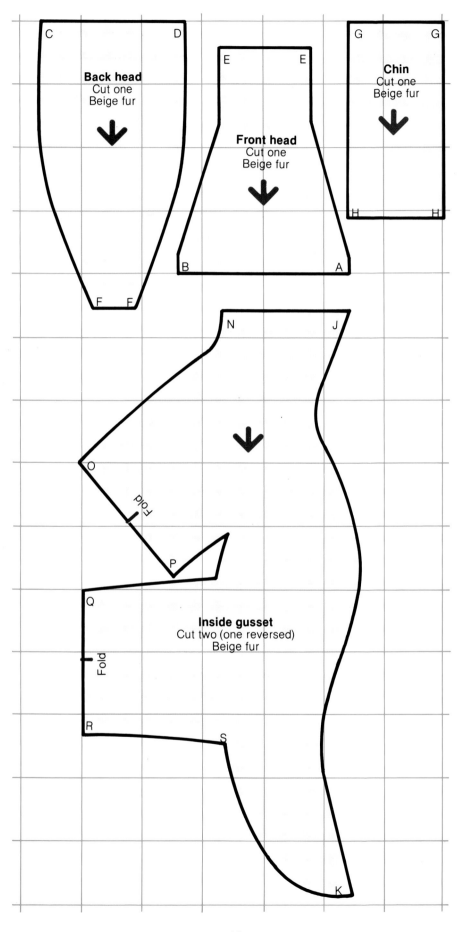

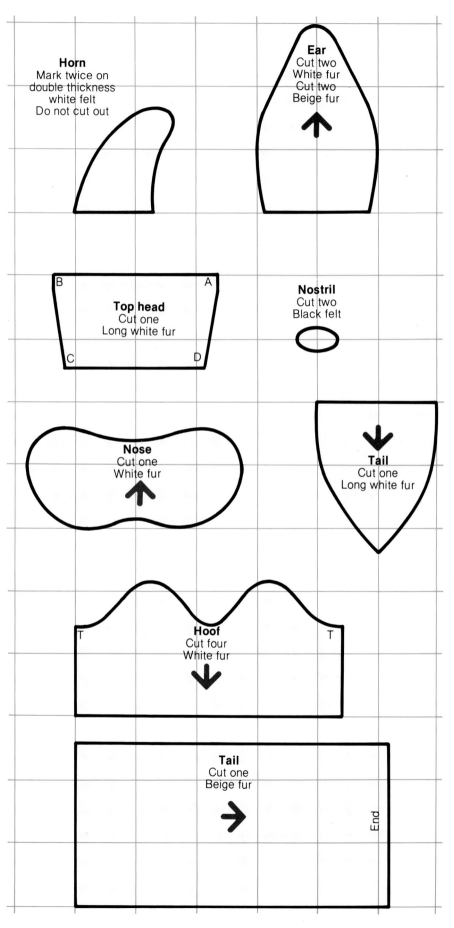

Horn
Mark twice on
double thickness
white felt
Do not cut out

Ear
Cut two
White fur
Cut two
Beige fur

B   A

Top head
Cut one
Long white fur

C   D

Nostril
Cut two
Black felt

Nose
Cut one
White fur

Tail
Cut one
Long white fur

T   T

Hoof
Cut four
White fur

Tail
Cut one
Beige fur

End

MATERIALS

25cm (10in) gold fur fabric
Small piece of dark brown felt
1 pair 13.5mm brown safety
* eyes with metal washers*
Thick black embroidery thread
Ribbon
Filling

With right sides together, join the two side head pieces by sewing seam G-H. Open out the head pieces and attach the head gusset, sewing from G to J on either side.

Pierce tiny holes for the eyes at the positions indicated and turn the head the right way out. Insert the eyes through the holes and secure on the reverse with washers. Stuff the head, starting with the nose. When the head is rounded, gather the raw edge of the neck using a running stitch and fasten off securely.

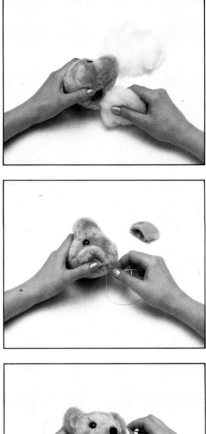

Sew the ear pieces together in pairs, leaving the bottom edge open. Turn the ears the right way out. Using strong thread, oversew the ears flat onto the head and then ladder stitch them along one side of the base so that they stand in an upright position.

Using thick black embroidery thread, embroider the nose on the bear using long straight stitches. Embroider the mouth with the same thread, then place the head to one side.

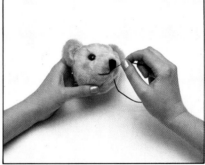

For the body, join the leg pieces to the body gusset by placing them with the right sides together and sewing from A to B on either side.

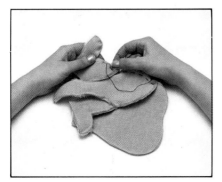

Keeping the right sides together, sew the gusset (with the attached legs) to the side piece from C to D, matching point A. Repeat for the other side. Then sew the base seams E-F, and finally sew the back seam C-F, leaving a gap for turning and filling.

Open out the raw edges of the feet. With the right sides together, place the foot pads against the raw edges of the feet and sew the pads into position. Make sure the narrow end is at the heel.

Turn the body the right way out and stuff gently, beginning with the toes. When the body is nicely rounded, close the gap with a ladder stitch. Then ladder stitch the head to the body, working around the head more than once. Finish off securely.

To make the arms, sew all the way around each pair. Cut a small slit at the inside top of each arm and turn the right way out through this slit. Stuff the arms gently, then oversew the slits. Ladder stitch the arms to the sides of the body, making sure they are attached securely. Tie a ribbon around the bear's neck, forming it into a bow.

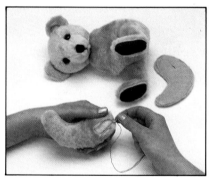

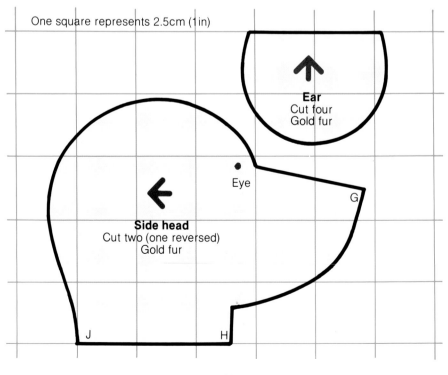

One square represents 2.5cm (1in)

Ear
Cut four
Gold fur

Eye

G

Side head
Cut two (one reversed)
Gold fur

J   H

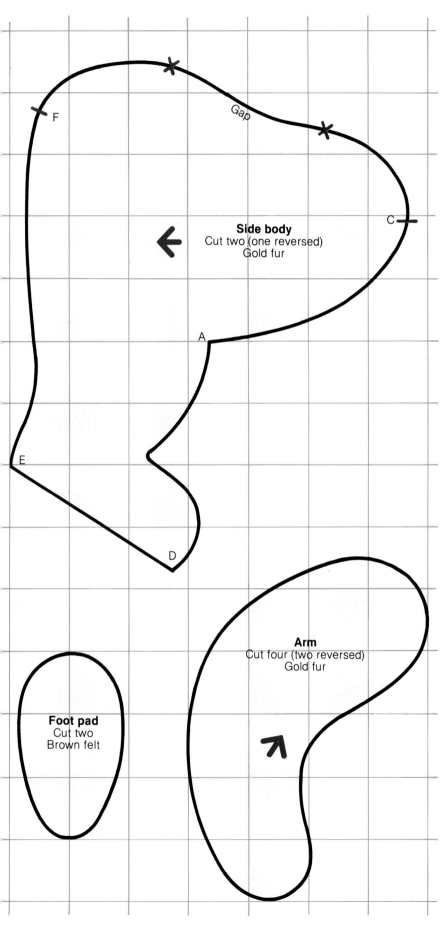

Side body
Cut two (one reversed)
Gold fur

Gap

F

C

A

E

D

Arm
Cut four (two reversed)
Gold fur

Foot pad
Cut two
Brown felt

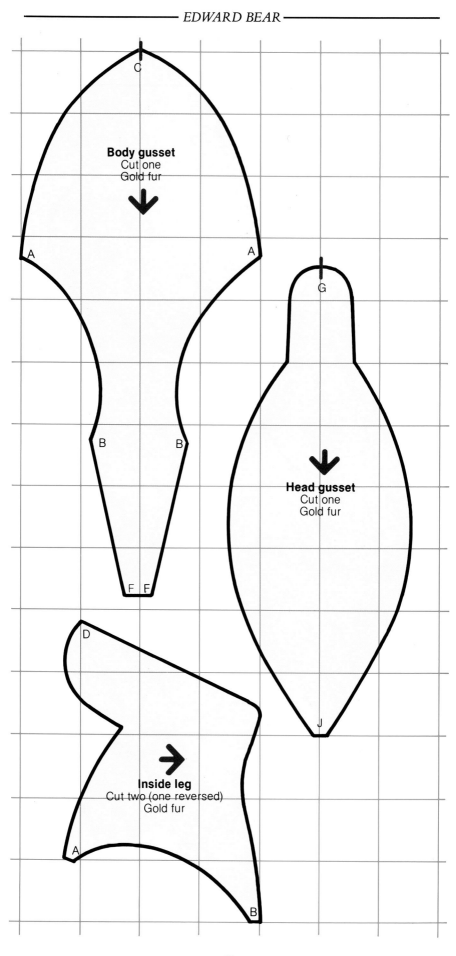

Body gusset
Cut one
Gold fur

Head gusset
Cut one
Gold fur

Inside leg
Cut two (one reversed)
Gold fur

MATERIALS

Striped jersey fabric
Small pieces of pink stockinette
Black felt for shoes and eyes
Blue denim fabric for trousers
64cm (26in) curly mohair for
  hair
Red ribbon
Red embroidery thread
Elastic
Filling

Using double layer fabric, sew a running stitch all the way around the head circle and begin to pull tight. Stuff the centre of the head as you are pulling the thread until the head is full and firm. Oversew and finish off firmly.

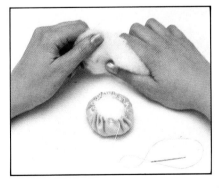

Using red embroidery thread, make two small stitches in a 'V' shape for the mouth. Cut two circles out of black felt for the eyes and sew into position on the face with a few small stitches.

Sew the two body pieces together, leaving the bottom straight edge open. Turn the body the right way out and fill with stuffing. Turning the raw edges in, close the base of the body. Place the body to one side.

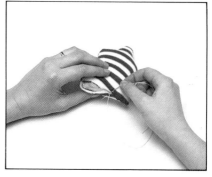

Join the short edges of the leg pieces to each shoe across the top. Fold the leg and shoe in half lengthwise and sew from the top of the leg to the bottom of the shoe, leaving the base open. Open out the base of the shoes and carefully sew in the shoe soles.

Turn the legs the right way out and stuff, ensuring that a good firm shape is maintained. Turn in the raw edges at the top of each leg. Keeping the seam at the centre, close the gap with a ladder stitch. Then oversew the tops of the legs to the base of the body using strong thread.

Fold the sleeve pieces in half lengthwise and sew from the bottom of the raw edge all the way around the top, rounding off the corners. Turn up a small hem and then place to one side. Fold the arm pieces in half lengthwise and sew around them, leaving the top straight edge open. Turn the arms the right way out and fill softly with stuffing.

Place the arm against the wrong side of the completed sleeve so the top edges are level. Oversew through all thicknesses, then pull the sleeves over the arms. Hold the completed arms against the body sides and sew into place at shoulder level. Place the head against the neck of the body, adjust the position and then ladder stitch firmly into place.

Take two lengths of mohair about 32cm (13in) long. Place one centrally across the top of the head. Starting at the centre forehead, back stitch the mohair firmly to the head. Add the second length of mohair at the back of the head and sew into place. Gather the hair at either side of the head and sew firmly onto the neck. Plait or braid the hair and add ribbons.

For the trousers, place the two pieces right sides together and sew seam A-B on one side only. Open out the two sides with the wrong side facing up. Turn up a small double hem on each leg. Turn down a double hem at the top edge to make a casing. Thread a piece of elastic through the casing so that it protrudes slightly on either side.

On one side, sew through the casing and elastic to hold in place. Pull the free end of elastic to gather the waist slightly and secure at the edge with a few stitches. Fold the trousers in half again and, with right sides together, sew the back seam A-B. Fold again so that the seams A-B meet in the middle. Sew seam C-B-C, then turn the trousers the right way out.

Fold the straps in half lengthwise. Fold the raw edges inside and sew along this edge. Sew the straps into position at the front and back of the trousers. Place the trousers on the doll, then turn up the bottoms of the legs twice.

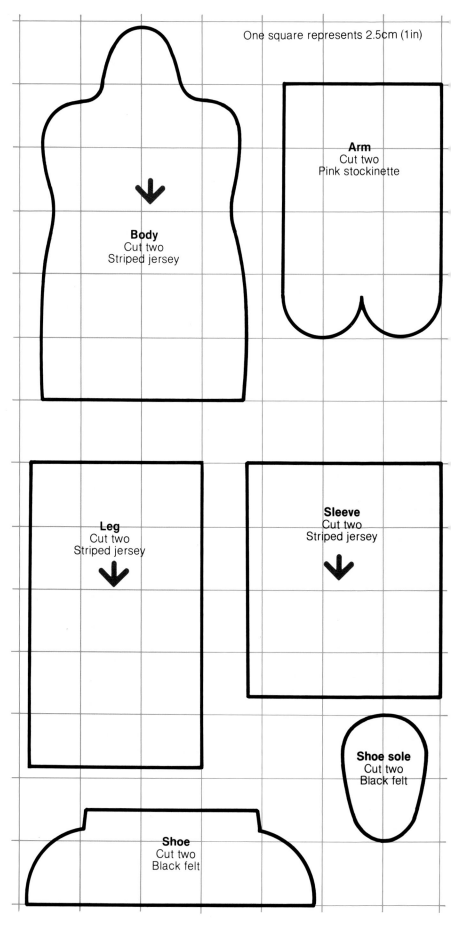

One square represents 2.5cm (1in)

Arm
Cut two
Pink stockinette

Body
Cut two
Striped jersey

Leg
Cut two
Striped jersey

Sleeve
Cut two
Striped jersey

Shoe sole
Cut two
Black felt

Shoe
Cut two
Black felt

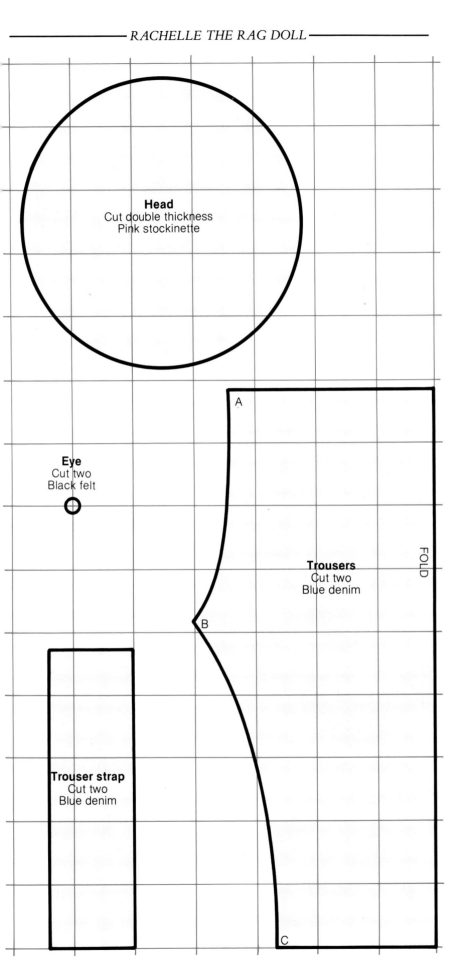

Head
Cut double thickness
Pink stockinette

Eye
Cut two
Black felt

A

Trousers
Cut two
Blue denim

FOLD

B

Trouser strap
Cut two
Blue denim

C

MATERIALS

Black fur fabric
White fur fabric
Small scraps of orange felt
Small scrap of white cotton
   fabric
Small piece of fabric for tie
1 pair of 13.5mm black
   safety eyes with washers
15cm (6in) length of elastic
Filling

Sew the wings to the linings, leaving the straight edges open. Turn wings the right way out, fold lengthwise (white inward) and oversew the top raw edge. Mark out the foot pattern twice onto a double layer of orange felt. Sew around these lines, leaving the straight edges open. Trim close to the stitches. Fill the feet with a small amount of stuffing.

With right sides together, sew seam A-B, joining the front to the side head pieces. Repeat with the other side. Place the two halves of the front head together and sew seam C-D. Place the head on the front body and sew seam E-D-E, matching the centre seam of the head with point D.

Referring to the positions indicated on the pattern, tack the feet and wings into position on the front body.

Sew seam F-G on the back body pieces, leaving a small gap in the centre for turning. Open out the back body and sew to the back head between H, F and H.

Place the back and front body right sides together. Sew all around, leaving the base open, and enclosing the wings in the seam at the positions indicated on the pattern. Sew the base to the body, matching point G at the tail and the centre front position. The feet should be enclosed in this seam.

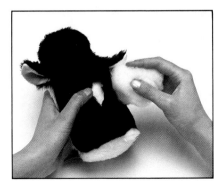

Pierce tiny holes at the eye positions on the head. Turn the penguin the right side out, poking out the tail. Insert the safety eyes through the holes and secure with metal washers. Stuff the penguin, starting with the head. Ensure the base is flat to allow the toy to stand upright and, when stuffed evenly, close the gap on the back body with a ladder stitch.

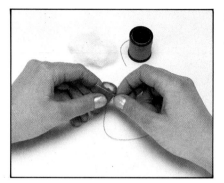

Sew the beak pieces together, leaving the straight edge open. Turn the beak and stuff. Using a running stitch, gather around the raw edge and pull tight. Ladder stitch the beak firmly into place on the head.

For the bow tie, cut a fabric strip 14cm x 4cm (5½in x 1½in). Fold the long edges over 12mm (½in), then the short edges into the middle to slightly overlap. Stitch through the centre of the tie, pleating it. Form a loop of elastic and stitch it to the tie. Cut a 4cm (1½in) square of fabric; fold in the raw edges, wrap around middle of tie and oversew at the back.

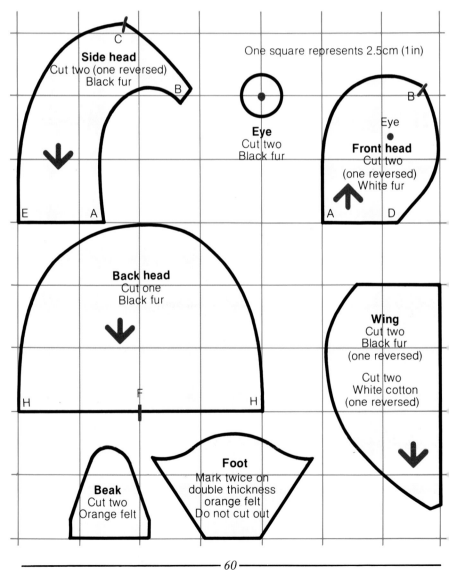

One square represents 2.5cm (1in)

Side head
Cut two (one reversed)
Black fur
C
B
E
A

Eye
Cut two
Black fur

Front head
Cut two
(one reversed)
White fur
B
Eye
A
D

Back head
Cut one
Black fur
H
F
H

Wing
Cut two
Black fur
(one reversed)

Cut two
White cotton
(one reversed)

Beak
Cut two
Orange felt

Foot
Mark twice on
double thickness
orange felt
Do not cut out

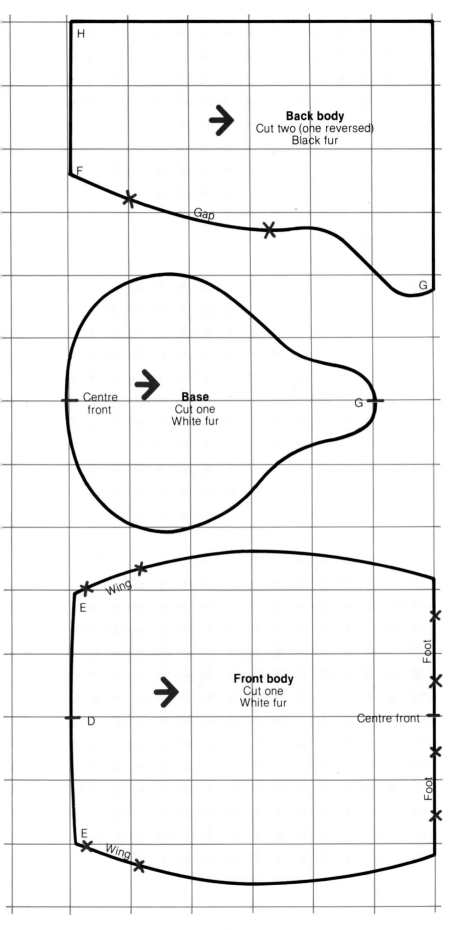

H

Back body
Cut two (one reversed)
Black fur

F

Gap

G

Centre
front

Base
Cut one
White fur

G

Wing

E

Foot

Front body
Cut one
White fur

D

Centre front

Foot

E

Wing

MATERIALS

Medium length glossy white fur
   fabric
Small piece of black felt
1 large square of white felt
Small piece of orange felt
1 pair 13.5mm black safety
   eyes with metal washers
Filling

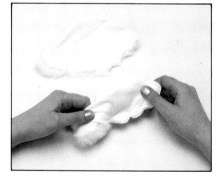

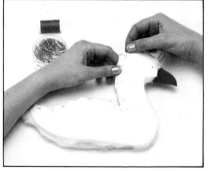

Make the wings for the adult swans by sewing the linings to the fur fabric pieces all around, leaving a small gap for turning. Turn the wings, pushing out the curves, and close the gap using a ladder stitch. Top stitch lines across the wings according to the pattern, to give the effect of feathers.

Attach the beak to either side of the body by sewing seam A-D. Place the two side body pieces right sides together and sew seam A-B, leaving a small gap at the rear of the neck for stuffing. Then sew seam D-C at the front of the neck.

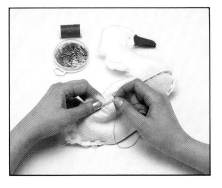

Open out the top body and sew to the base, matching points C and B. Leave a gap as shown on one side of the body only. Using orange thread, sew around the beak from the top to the bottom.

Pierce tiny holes for the eyes at the position indicated, then turn the swan the right way out through the gap at the base. Insert the safety eyes through the holes and secure on the reverse side of the head with the metal washers.

Start to fill the swan at the beak tip, using the gap at the rear of the neck for access. Once the head and neck are filled, close the neck gap. Continue to fill the body cavity and then close the gap at the base. Oversew each wing to the body sides of the adult swans in a small triangle around the wing base.

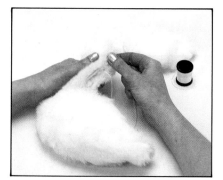

Oversew the black felt 'knob' pieces together around the curved end. Turn the right way out and fill the rounded part with a tiny amount of stuffing. Wrap the knob around the base of the adult swan's beak and oversew the ends together under the beak. Secure the knob around the head with a few small stitches.

Using black thread, sew a straight line along the swan's beak on either side. Alternatively, use a waterproof, non-toxic felt tip pen to draw the line. Embroider or draw nostrils on each side of the beak.

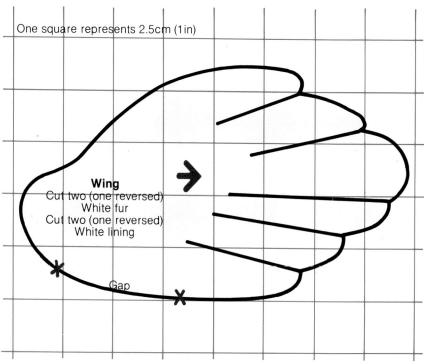

One square represents 2.5cm (1in)

Wing
Cut two (one reversed)
White fur
Cut two (one reversed)
White lining

Gap

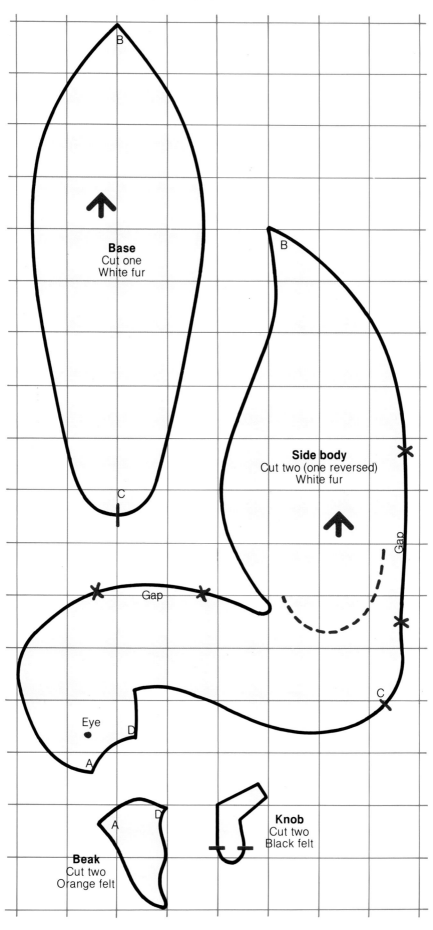

Base
Cut one
White fur

Side body
Cut two (one reversed)
White fur

Gap

Gap

Eye

Knob
Cut two
Black felt

Beak
Cut two
Orange felt

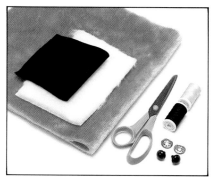

MATERIALS

Small scrap of honey-coloured fur
Small scrap of long-haired white fur
Scrap of black felt
1 pair 13.5mm brown safety eyes with washers
Filling

Place the side head pieces right sides together and sew seam A-B. Open out the head and sew the gusset to the head, starting at point A, matching points C and around to D. Repeat on the other side.

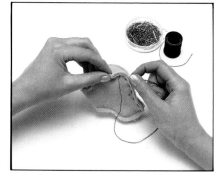

Pierce tiny holes for the eyes in the head, then turn the head the right way out. Put in the safety eyes, securing on the reverse side with metal washers. Stuff the head then, using a running stitch, gather the raw edge together tightly and finish off.

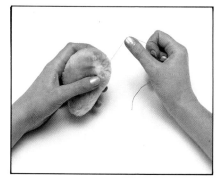

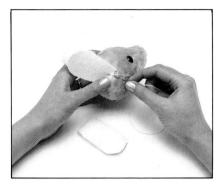

Using the white fur, carefully cut the two ears and position as shown, just beneath the gusset seam. Oversew the ears to the top of the head. Sew a couple of stitches to hold the ears in position.

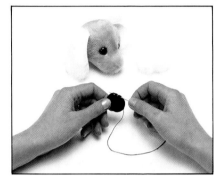

Using a running stitch, gather the raw edge of the nose. Place a little stuffing in the centre of the nose and pull the thread tight. Oversew a few times, then ladder stitch the nose into position on the puppy's head.

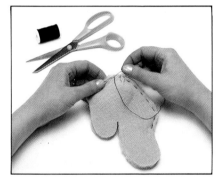

Sew the darts together on both side body pieces. Place the two body pieces right sides together and sew seam E-F.

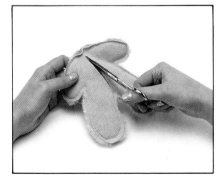

Open out the body and place against the underbody with the right sides together. Sew the body to the underbody, matching points E and F. Cut a slit along the centre of the base.

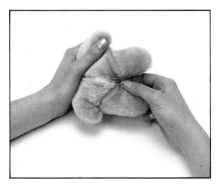

Turn and stuff the body. Close the gap with a ladder stitch. Fold the tail lengthwise and sew, leaving the straight edge open. Turn and fold the raw edges in at the end. Ladder stitch to the rear of the puppy at right angles to the back seam. Place the head on the body in a slightly tilted position and ladder stitch into position several times around.

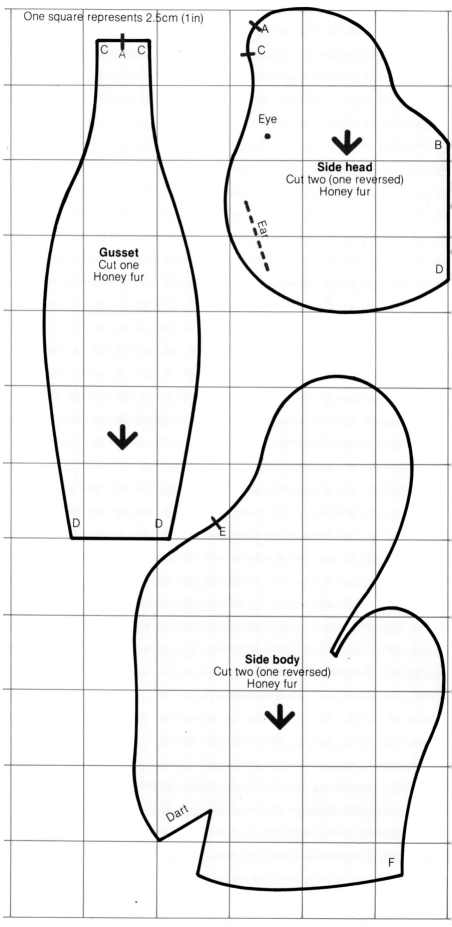

One square represents 2.5cm (1in)

C A C

A
C

Eye

B

Side head
Cut two (one reversed)
Honey fur

Ear

D

Gusset
Cut one
Honey fur

D D

E

Side body
Cut two (one reversed)
Honey fur

Dart

F

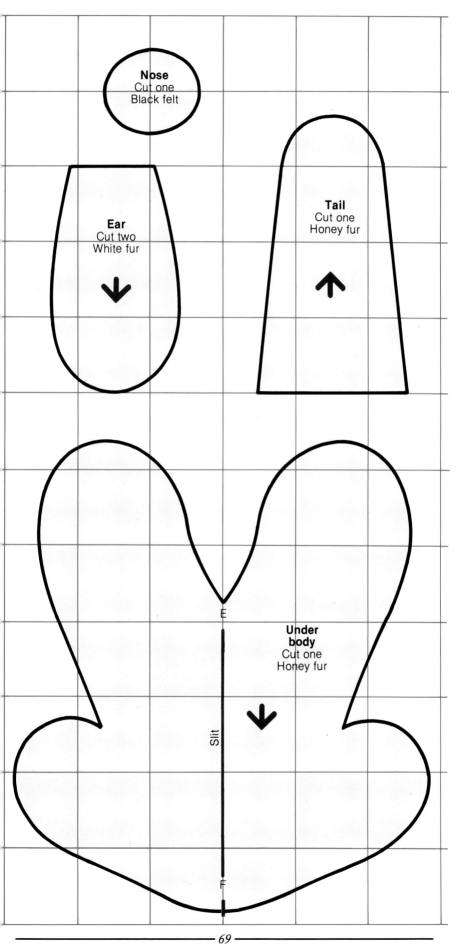

Nose
Cut one
Black felt

Ear
Cut two
White fur

Tail
Cut one
Honey fur

E

Under body
Cut one
Honey fur

Slit

F

MATERIALS

Small piece of black or white fur
  fabric
Scrap of pink or white felt
1 pair 13.5mm green safety
  eyes with washers
Filling
Pink embroidery thread

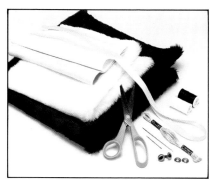

Place the two side head pieces right sides together and sew between points C and D. Then sew the two back head pieces together along seam A-B.

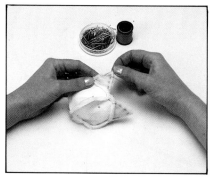

Pierce tiny holes in the fabric at the eye positions. Sew the ear lining to the side of the head on both sides between E and F. Place the back and front head pieces together and sew all around the head, leaving a small gap at the base for turning and filling.

Turn the head the right way out, carefully easing out the tips of the ears. Flatten the ears and sew across the seam through all thicknesses of fabric. Insert the safety eyes, securing them with the metal washers.

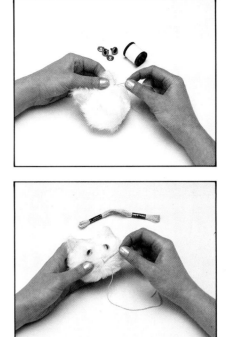

Fill the head with stuffing, easing it into a round shape. Sew a running stitch around the raw edges of the head. Pull it tight and finish off at the base. Embroider a small pink nose, referring to the instructions on page 17.

With right sides together, join the body gussets together between G and H, leaving a gap for turning. Join the gusset to the side body along seams G-K, H-J, and L-M. Repeat on the other side.

Fold the tail in half lengthwise, wrong sides together, and sew along the edge. Trim close to the seam and turn the right way out. Give the tail a gentle pull to improve the shape. Sew the back of the body between G and H, inserting the tail into position at the same time.

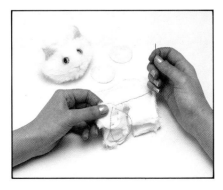

Sew the pads into the base of the feet. Turn the body the right way out and stuff gently. Close the gap with a ladder stitch. Join the head to the body firmly with a ladder stitch, working around the head twice.

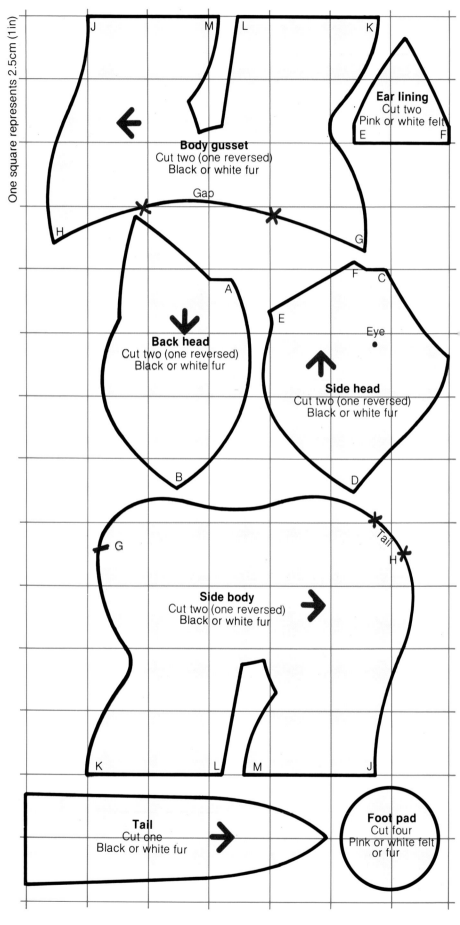

One square represents 2.5cm (1in)

Body gusset
Cut two (one reversed)
Black or white fur

Gap

Ear lining
Cut two
Pink or white felt

Back head
Cut two (one reversed)
Black or white fur

Eye

Side head
Cut two (one reversed)
Black or white fur

Side body
Cut two (one reversed)
Black or white fur

Tail

Tail
Cut one
Black or white fur

Foot pad
Cut four
Pink or white felt
or fur

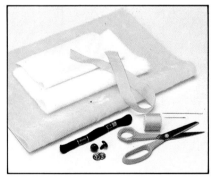

MATERIALS

Piece of lemon fur fabric
Scraps of white cotton fabric for
ear lining
Small scrap of white fur for tail
1 pair 13.5mm brown safety
eyes with washers
Black embroidery thread
Ribbon
Filling

Sew the puppet's ears to the linings, leaving the straight edge open. Turn ears the right way out. Cut slits on both head pieces for ears and pierce tiny holes for the eyes. Fold the completed ears lengthwise (with lining innermost) and, with the lining facing forward, push into the slits. Sew on the wrong side through all layers of fabric.

Join the two sides of the head together from A to B, leaving the straight edge open. Turn the head the right way out. Insert the safety eyes in the holes made earlier and secure with metal washers. Softly fill the head, adding a bit at a time, creating a central hole through to the top of the head. (A thick felt-tip pen can be used to form the hole.)

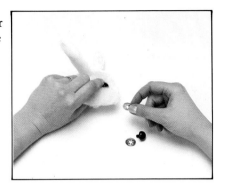

Place the two halves of the body right sides together and sew all around, leaving the bottom straight edge open. Turn up a hem of about 1cm (½in) around the base and sew. Turn the body the right way out.

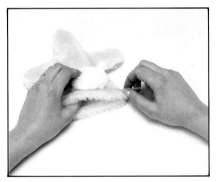

Using a running stitch, gather the raw edge of the tail piece. Pull together and fasten off. Place on the body and ladder stitch into position.

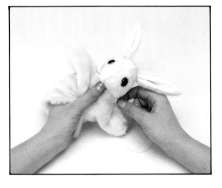

Place the body onto your hand, with your forefinger in the top; then push your finger into the head as far as it will go. Ladder stitch the head to the body, folding in the raw edge at the same time.

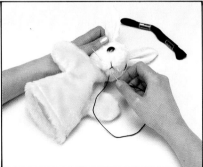

Using black embroidery thread, embroider a nose on the puppet referring to the instructions on page 17. Sew a couple of stitches from the base of each ear to the head to hold the ears in an upright position. Tie a bright ribbon around the rabbit's neck and fill the body with Easter eggs or sweets to make a gift for a child.

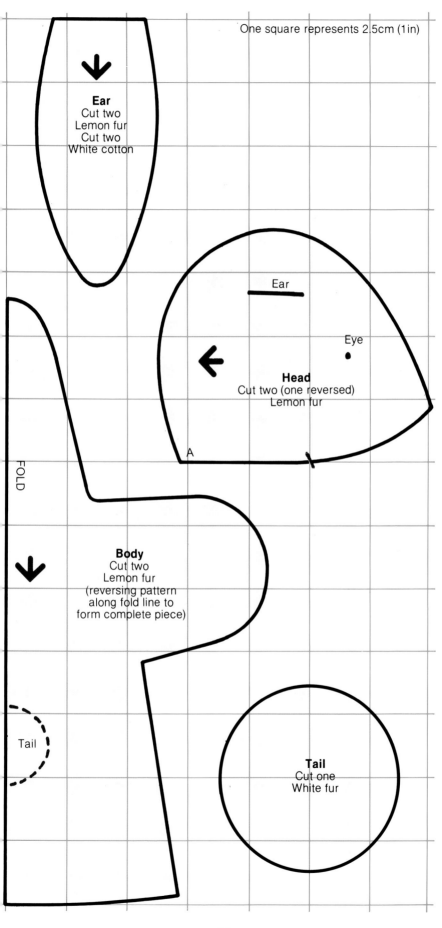

One square represents 2.5cm (1in)

Ear
Cut two
Lemon fur
Cut two
White cotton

Ear

Eye

Head
Cut two (one reversed)
Lemon fur

A

FOLD

Body
Cut two
Lemon fur
(reversing pattern
along fold line to
form complete piece)

Tail

Tail
Cut one
White fur

MATERIALS

Red velvet or felt
Square of white felt
Scrap of self-adhesive black felt
Pink stockinette
1 ball of brown wool for hair
About 1m (1yd) of 2cm (¾in) ribbon
Small piece of narrow red ribbon
2 small poms poms
Red and white embroidery thread
Filling

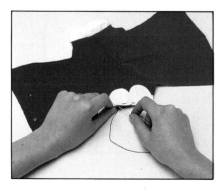

With right sides together, join the two side back pieces of the puppet from A to B. Open out and sew to the front piece across the top along C-Λ-C. Open out the front and back. Gather some ribbon into frills and tack into place along straight edge D-C-D. Place the hand piece along this edge and, with straight edges together, sew along D-C-D through all thicknesses.

Fold the front and back body over again so that the right sides are together. Then, join the side seams from the curve of the hand down to point E, changing thread colour as necessary. Turn up a small hem at the bottom of the puppet and place to one side.

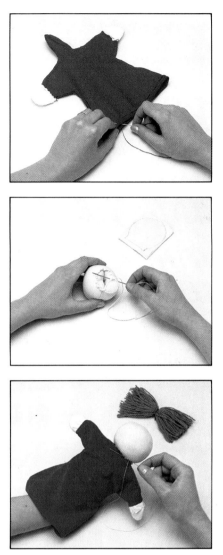

Mark out the head shape onto four layers of stockinette. Sew and then cut around the shape. Turn the head the right way out, with two layers on either side of the central hole. Fill the cavities on both sides equally, leaving the middle hole empty. Oversew the raw edges to hold the filling in place, but leave the centre area open.

Push the neck of the puppet body into the middle hole of the head so that the head is level with the arms. Neatly sew the head into position all around. Take a small bundle of wool roughly 15cm (6in) long and tie in the middle with strong thread. Sew the centre of the bundle to the top of the head and spread out the hair. Cut a little at the front for a fringe.

To make the hat, fold the double thickness felt hat shape in half and sew along the straight edge through all layers. Turn the right way out. Gather some more ribbon into a frill and oversew this around the hat base. Stitch two tiny ribbon bows to the front of the hat. Place the hat firmly on the top of the head and sew into position through the wool hair and onto the head itself.

Sew two red crosses at the eye positions and a small red V for the mouth. Cut eyes out of black felt and stick them to the centre of each cross. Sew two black stitches to the middle of each eye. Sew a tiny stitch with white thread to highlight each eye. Make a ribbon frill to fit the neck and secure it tightly at the back. Sew pom poms down the front of the puppet.

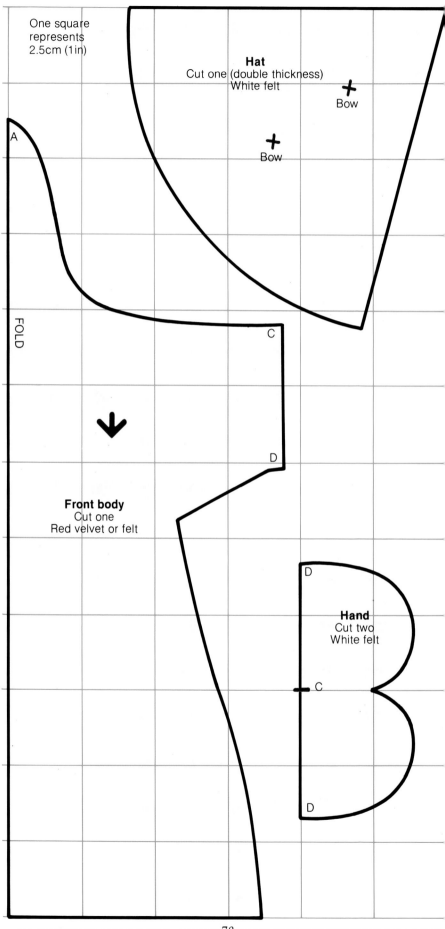

One square
represents
2.5cm (1in)

Hat
Cut one (double thickness)
White felt

Bow

Bow

A

FOLD

C

D

Front body
Cut one
Red velvet or felt

D

Hand
Cut two
White felt

C

D

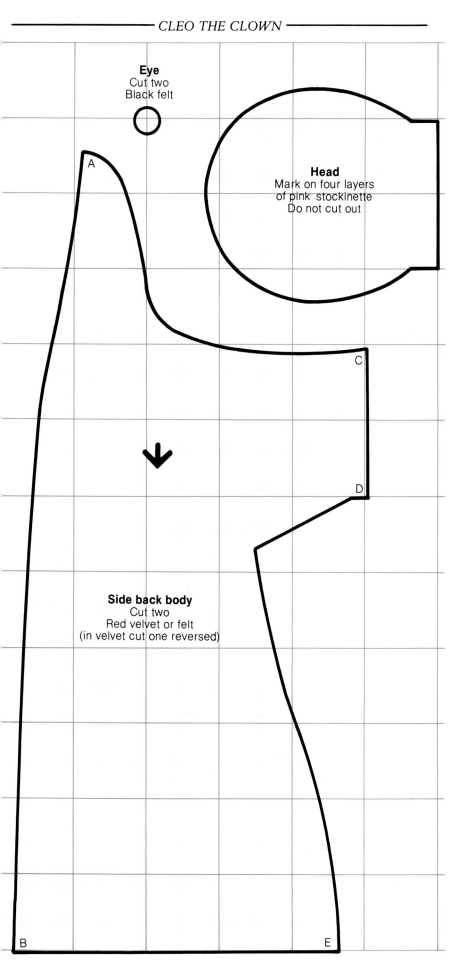

Eye
Cut two
Black felt

Head
Mark on four layers
of pink stockinette
Do not cut out

A

C

D

Side back body
Cut two
Red velvet or felt
(in velvet cut one reversed)

B

E

MATERIALS

Flesh coloured felt
Green felt
Black felt or suede fabric for
  boots
Black velvet or felt for dress
Black velvet for hat
40cm (16in) ribbon
Thick black thread
Pink embroidery thread
Filling

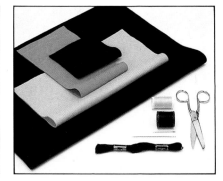

Mark out the side head piece of the puppet onto two layers of flesh coloured felt. Sew along the line from the top of the head to the neck edge, around the profile of the nose and chin. Cut around the entire head with scissors, snipping very carefully between the nose and chin up to the seam.

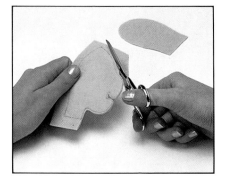

Open out the head piece and, with right sides together, sew to the back head piece, leaving the bottom straight edge open.

Turn the head the right way out, poking out the nose and chin gently. Fill the head, starting with the nose and chin. Add a little more filling, then ensure that a central cavity is formed. (A thick felt-tip pen can be used to form the hole.) Place the head to one side.

To join the two side dress pieces, place them right sides together and sew seam A-B. Open the pieces out and sew to the front dress piece across the top along C-A-C.

Open out the arms and sew the hand pieces to the dress between points D, C and D along the straight edge. Fold the arms back again and sew together from the tip of the hand down to the base of the dress between points E and F. Turn up a small hem on the lower edge and sew, then turn the puppet the right way out.

Push the 'neck' of the dress into the head cavity firmly, inserting it as far as possible. Then ladder stitch the head to the body with small stitches. Sew a mouth on the head using black thread, referring to the photograph. Stitch black beady eyes and pull together slightly with a long needle. Finish off the face by sewing two eyebrows, using only a couple of stitches.

Place the hair piece on the head. Fold the back and sides down, then sew into place around the crown. Cut the felt into ribbons to give a hair effect.

Turn and sew a single hem along the curved edge of the hat. Fold the hat in half with right sides together and sew the long edge, leaving the base open. Pull the hat onto the head over the hair. Stitch around the base, keeping the seam at the back, through all layers of hat, hair and head material.

Place the two hat brim circles right sides together and sew around the outer edge. Turn the brim the right way out and top stitch around the edge of the brim and around the centre raw edge. Pull the hat brim down over the top of the hat, bringing the raw edge level with the base of the peak. Stitch into place all around the head.

Conceal the raw edge of the hat with a strip of black felt. Fold down the point of the hat about 2cm (¾in) from the top and catch in place on the side of the hat with a couple of small stitches.

Using a running stitch, gather the centre of a 40cm (16in) piece of ribbon. Place the ribbon around the witch's neck and adjust the gathers to fit. Join the ribbon at the back of the neck and fasten off tightly.

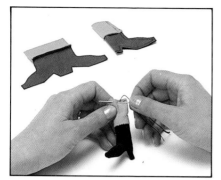

To make the shoes, sew the green felt rectangles to the black boot pieces along the straight edge. Fold in half and sew all around, leaving the top edge open. Turn the right way out, taking care to push out the toe tips. Stuff the boots a little at a time. Fold the top of the legs so that the seams are at the centre and sew under the bottom hem of the dress.

Shoe laces can be added if desired, using thick black embroidery thread. Add a wart or two to the witch's nose and chin by sewing a large French knot with thick pink embroidery thread.

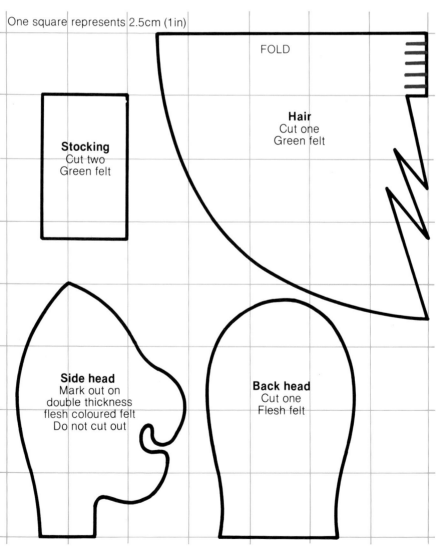

One square represents 2.5cm (1in)

FOLD

Hair
Cut one
Green felt

Stocking
Cut two
Green felt

Side head
Mark out on
double thickness
flesh coloured felt
Do not cut out

Back head
Cut one
Flesh felt

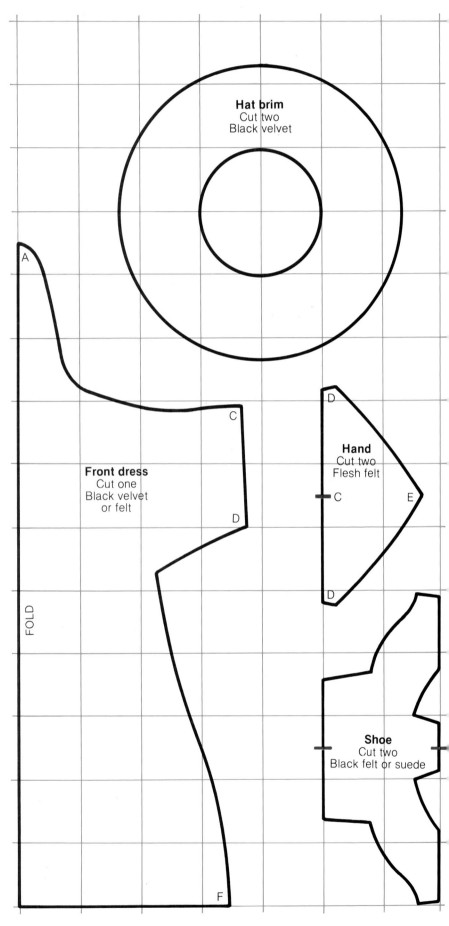

Hat brim
Cut two
Black velvet

Front dress
Cut one
Black velvet
or felt

FOLD

A

C

D

F

Hand
Cut two
Flesh felt

D

C

E

D

Shoe
Cut two
Black felt or suede

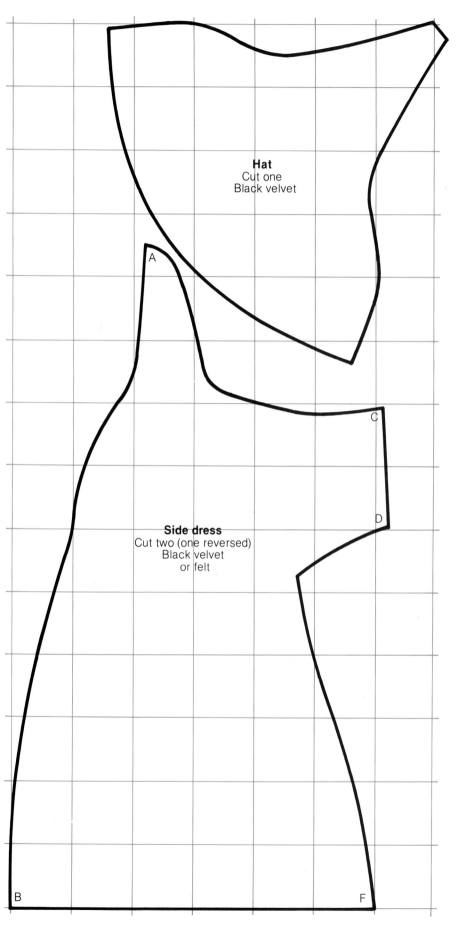

Hat
Cut one
Black velvet

A

C

D

Side dress
Cut two (one reversed)
Black velvet
or felt

B

F

GEORGE THE DRAGON

MATERIALS

2 large squares of green felt
2 large squares of orange felt
Tiny scrap of black felt
Tiny scrap of white felt
Black embroidery thread
White embroidery thread
·Filling

Sew the orange linings onto the puppet's green ears, leaving the straight edges open. Turn ears the right way out and fold in half, with the orange facing inwards. Cut slits in the side head pieces and push the raw edges of the ears through the slits. Sew on the reverse side to secure.

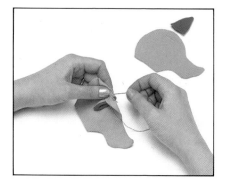

With the right sides together, sew the side head pieces together from J to K. Then join the gusset to the side head pieces from J to L on either side, leaving the bottom edge open.

Turn the head the right way out. Start filling the head at the nose, adding a little bit of stuffing at a time. Make sure that a central cavity remains in the head for the finger. (You can use a thick felt-tip pen to form the cavity.)

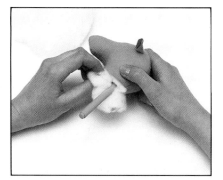

Sew the wings together, leaving the straight edges open. Turn the wings the right way out. Cut slits in the side body pieces and push the raw edges of the wings into the slits. Sew the wings into position on the reverse. Turn the side bodies over with the wings facing up. Fold the wings back and top stitch down to the body about 5mm (¼in) from the edge.

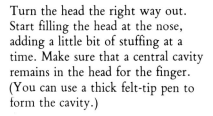

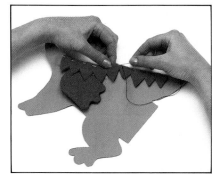

Tack the straight edges of the back ridge pieces along the right side body piece between the notches. Place the other side body piece on top and sew through all thicknesses of fabric, starting at point A around to point B.

Place the two front body pieces together and sew close to the edge all around, leaving the straight edge at the bottom open. Fill with a small amount of stuffing, easing it out evenly over the entire area. Starting between points C and C, sew straight lines across the body, about 25mm (1in) apart, through all layers of fabric all the way down the front.

With the right sides together, sew the inside arms and inside legs to the front body, sewing seam C-D and seam E-F on either side.

Open out the back body and, starting at point A, sew the front body to the back right around the arms and legs to point G. Repeat on other side. Sew the dart at the front body base and turn up a single hem. Turn the body the right way out. Fill the feet and legs with a little stuffing and top stitch along the base of the leg through all thicknesses of fabric.

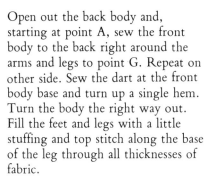

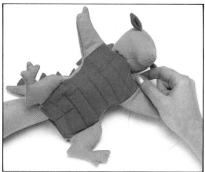

Push the forefinger part of the puppet up into the head as far as it will go. Ladder stitch the head to the body all the way around several times, using strong thread.

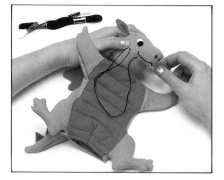

Sew eye pieces to the head with black embroidery thread. Using the same thread, add eyelashes and eyebrows. Then embroider the nostrils and mouth as shown in the photograph. With white embroidery thread, sew a few stitches at the front of the mouth to suggest teeth.

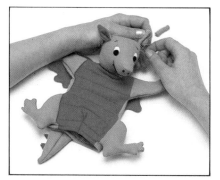

Take the felt horn pieces and roll them tightly into tubes. Oversew along the free edge to secure the horns, then ladder stitch firmly to the head at the side of the ears.

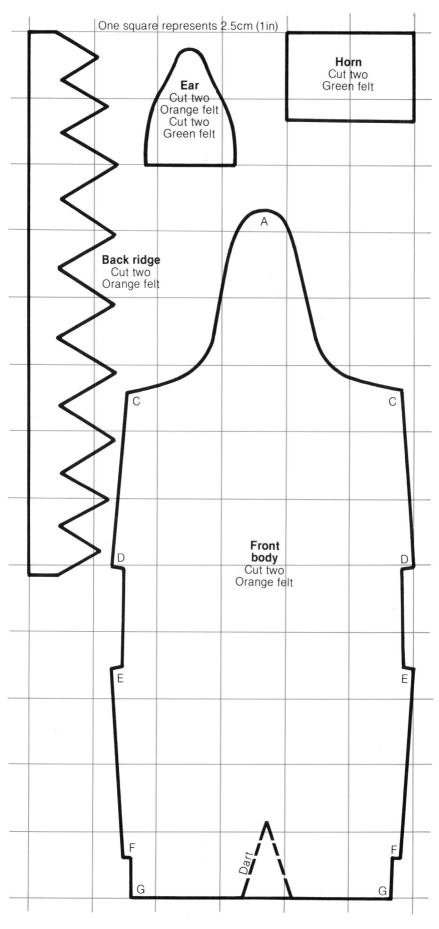

One square represents 2.5cm (1in)

Ear
Cut two
Orange felt
Cut two
Green felt

Horn
Cut two
Green felt

Back ridge
Cut two
Orange felt

A

C

C

D

D

Front body
Cut two
Orange felt

E

E

F

F

Dart

G

G

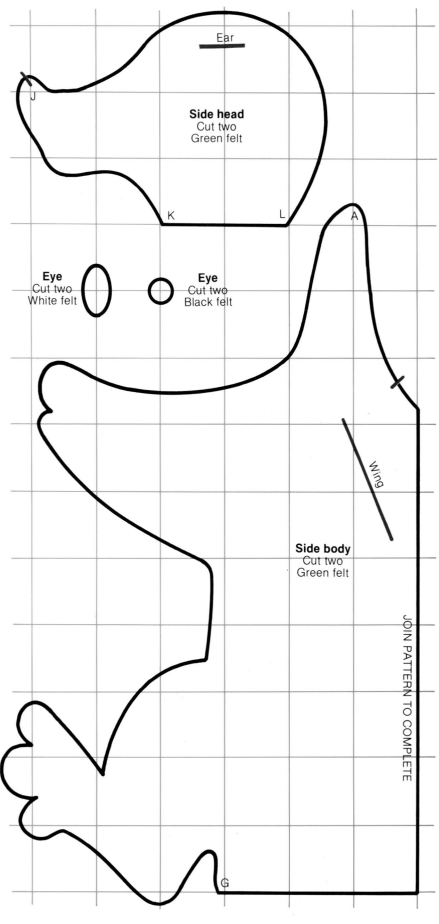

Ear

Side head
Cut two
Green felt

J

K   L   A

Eye
Cut two
White felt

Eye
Cut two
Black felt

Wing

Side body
Cut two
Green felt

JOIN PATTERN TO COMPLETE

G

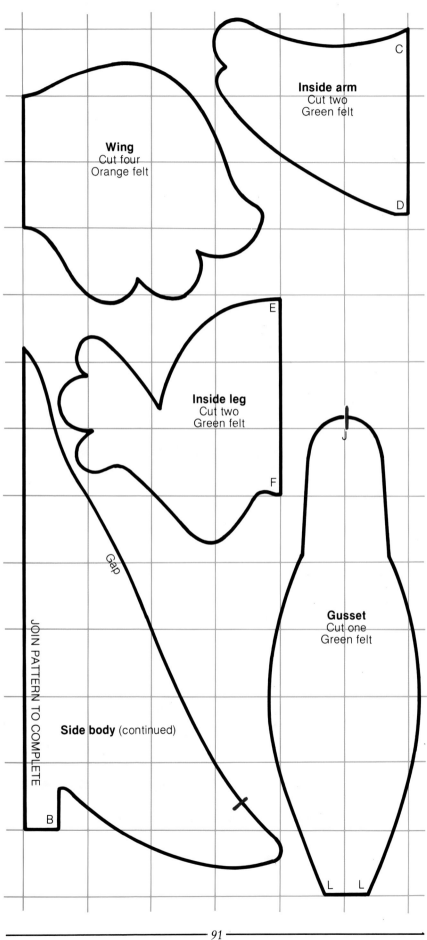

Inside arm
Cut two
Green felt

C

D

Wing
Cut four
Orange felt

E

Inside leg
Cut two
Green felt

F

J

Gusset
Cut one
Green felt

Gap

JOIN PATTERN TO COMPLETE

Side body (continued)

B

L   L

MATERIALS

Red velvet or felt
Black felt
Pink or flesh coloured felt
Very long white fur fabric
Short white fur fabric, for
   pom pom
Ribbon
Filling

For the body, sew the inside legs to the front body from A to B on either side. With right sides together, join the front body with attached legs to the side body from point D to C, matching point B. Repeat for the other side.

Open out the leg seams and sew the boot to the leg along E-D-E. Then fold the boot with right sides facing and sew the front to the side body along seam G-E on both sides, ensuring that point A matches. Sew seam E-F in black thread.

Close the back seam from G to C, leaving a gap for turning. Sew the boot soles into place. Turn the body the right way out and stuff firmly. Ladder stitch the back opening closed and place the body to one side.

For the jacket, join the two halves together by sewing seam L-M-L. Sew the sleeves to the jacket along J-K-J, easing to fit. Sew a strip of white fur fabric 14cm x 4cm (5½in x 1½in) to the edge of the sleeves, keeping the right sides together. Fold the strip over the raw edge of the sleeve and sew down on the reverse side.

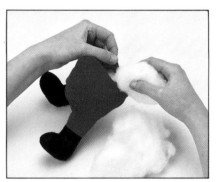

Fold the sleeves in half and sew up the side seam O-J-N on both sides. At the base of the jacket, sew a strip of white fur fabric 42cm x 4cm (16½in x 1½in). Fold the strip back over the raw edge of the jacket and sew into place on the reverse side.

For the hood, turn up a narrow double hem on each short side. Sew a strip of white fur fabric 23cm x 4cm (9¼in x 1½in) to the front edge in the same way as for the jacket. Fold the hood in half and, with right sides together, sew seam P-Q.

Turn the hood the right way out and add a short piece of ribbon to each front corner of the hood. Fold down the point of the hood. Sew a running stitch around the edge of the pom pom and gather. Stuff gently, then pull the thread to gather tightly. Attach the pom pom to the side of the hood.

Place the pairs of arms right sides together and sew all around, leaving the top straight edges open. Turn and stuff the arms, then oversew arms to the body sides. Place the jacket on the body.

To make the head, sew up the darts on both head pieces. Place the two halves together with right sides facing and sew around the head, leaving the bottom straight edge open.

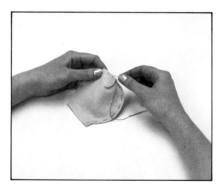

Turn the head the right way out. Place some filling into the head, stuffing it firmly. Gather the bottom edge of the head with a running stitch, then ladder stitch the head to the body.

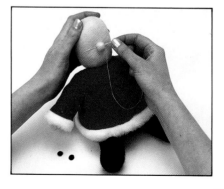

Using a running stitch, gather the edge of the nose. Place a small amount of filling in the centre, then fasten off securely. Stitch the nose to the centre of the face. Cut two eye circles out of black felt and sew them into position above the nose.

Fold the side flaps of the long white hair piece down and sew seam R-S on either side. Sew the beard to the front of the hair piece from T to U on both sides. Turn the right way out and pull onto Santa's head so that the top of the beard just touches the nose. Stitch into place. Put the hood on Santa's head and tie into place under the beard.

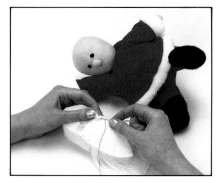

One square represents 2.5cm (1in)

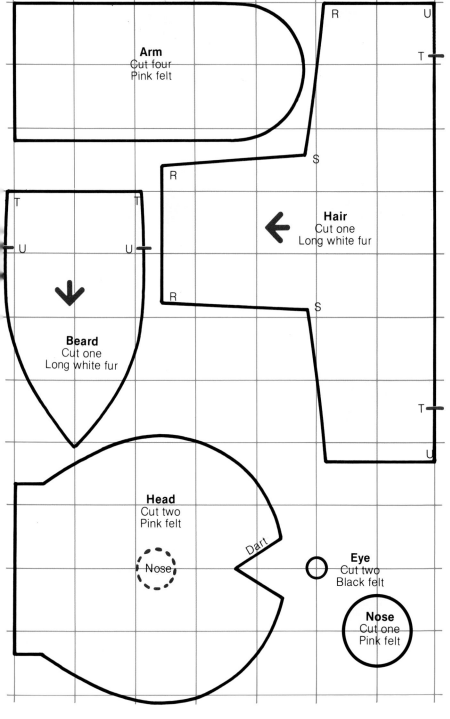

Arm
Cut four
Pink felt

R   U

T

S

R

Hair
Cut one
Long white fur

T   T

U   U

R

S

Beard
Cut one
Long white fur

T

U

Head
Cut two
Pink felt

Nose

Dart

Eye
Cut two
Black felt

Nose
Cut one
Pink felt

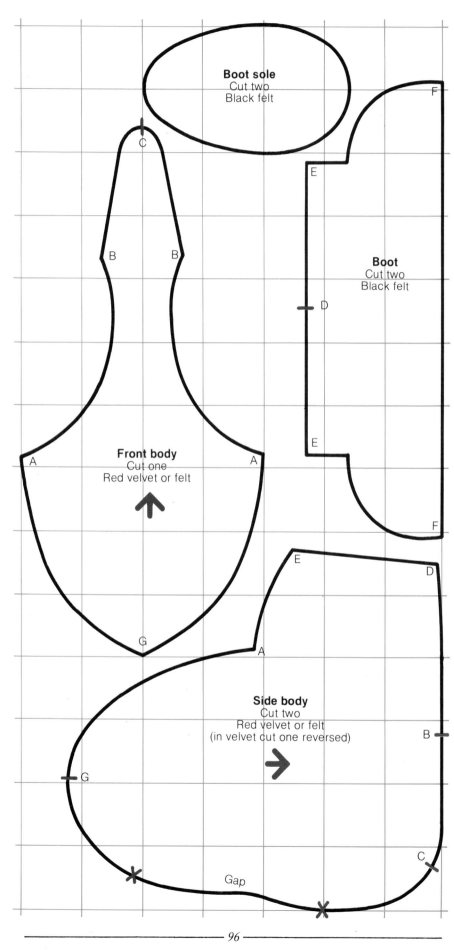

Boot sole
Cut two
Black felt

C

B B

Boot
Cut two
Black felt

D

E

F

E

F

Front body
Cut one
Red velvet or felt

A A

G

E D

A

Side body
Cut two
Red velvet or felt
(in velvet cut one reversed)

B

G

C

Gap

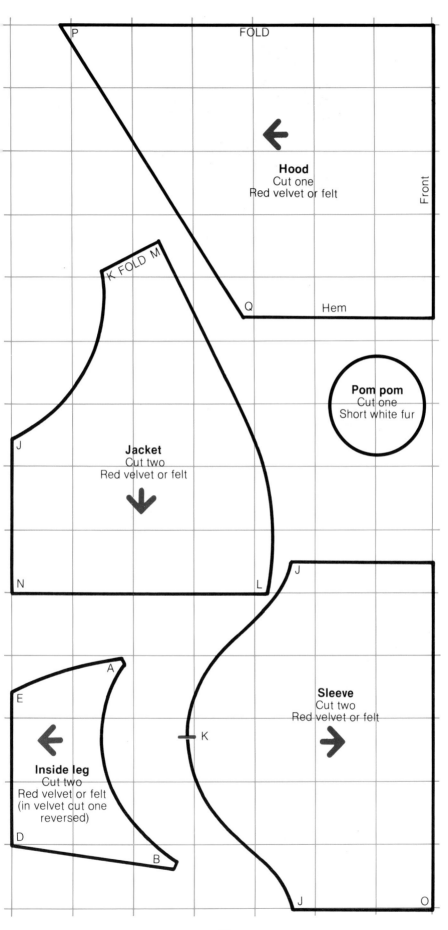

P

FOLD

Hood
Cut one
Red velvet or felt

Front

K FOLD M

Q   Hem

Pom pom
Cut one
Short white fur

J

Jacket
Cut two
Red velvet or felt

N   L

J

A

E

Sleeve
Cut two
Red velvet or felt

K

Inside leg
Cut two
Red velvet or felt
(in velvet cut one
reversed)

D

B

J   O

MATERIALS

Short pile white fur fabric
Black, red and green felt
Scrap of orange felt for nose
1 pair 13.5mm black safety
    eyes with metal washers
Black embroidery thread
Filling

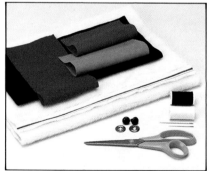

Make up the snowman body using
the same method as for Santa's body
(see pages 92/93). Use white fur for
the body and black felt for the feet.
Stuff the body well, making it fat
and rounded; place to one side. Sew
dart on each of the head pieces. Then
place the two halves right sides
together and sew around the head,
leaving the bottom straight edge
open.

Pierce tiny holes in the eye positions and turn the head the right way out. Insert the safety eyes in the holes and secure on the reverse with metal washers. Stuff the head, shaping it into a round fat ball. Using a running stitch, gather the raw edge at the base and finish off securely.

Fold the nose piece in half and sew along the straight edge. Turn the right way out and stuff firmly. Gather the raw edge of the nose and finish off. Place this end on head at a central position between the eyes and ladder stitch firmly into place. Using black embroidery thread, stitch a 'V'-shaped mouth below the eyes. Then ladder stitch the head to the body.

Place each pair of arms right sides together and sew all around, leaving the top straight edges open. Turn the arms the right way out and stuff them, adding far less filling to the top halves. Turn the raw edges in and oversew the arms into position on either side of the neck. Secure the hands to the body with a couple of stitches.

Sew the two hat brim pieces together around both the outer and inner edges. Fold the main body of the hat in half and sew around the short edge. Place the completed cylinder on top of the hat brim in a central position and oversew the two pieces together around the inner circle. Oversew the hat top into position and put some filling inside the hat.

Put the hat on the head in a lopsided position and stitch down. Wrap a red felt strip 19cm x 2cm (7½in x ¾in) around the base of the hat. Overlap ends and sew into place. Sew holly leaves onto the hat and buttons onto the body. Cut a red or green felt strip 5cm x 40cm (2in x 16in). Fringe the ends and tie scarf around the snowman's neck.

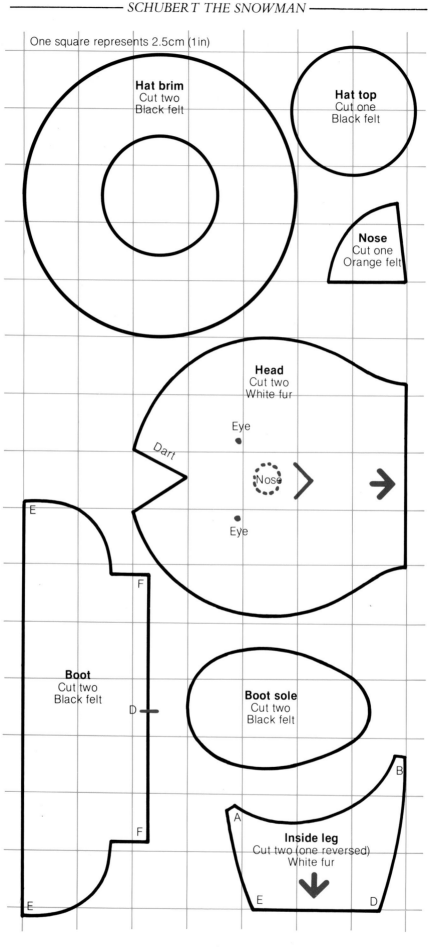

One square represents 2.5cm (1in)

Hat brim
Cut two
Black felt

Hat top
Cut one
Black felt

Nose
Cut one
Orange felt

Head
Cut two
White fur

Eye

Dart

Nose

Eye

E

F

Boot
Cut two
Black felt

D

Boot sole
Cut two
Black felt

F

B

A

Inside leg
Cut two (one reversed)
White fur

E

D

E

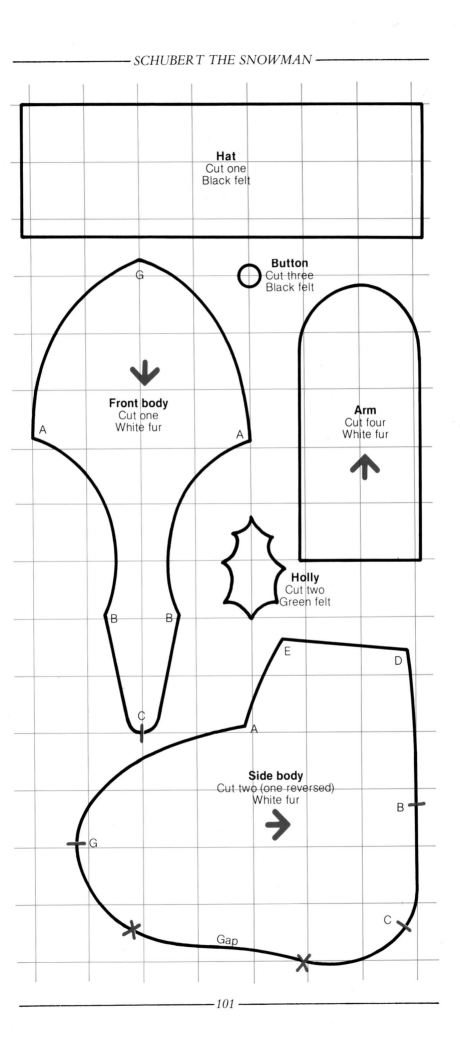

MATERIALS

30cm x 150cm (12in x 60in)
  grey felt, velvet or suede
  fabric
Piece of pink fabric (i.e. velvet)
  for ear lining and feet
3 pairs 12mm safety eyes
  with metal washers
Filling

Clothing

Small piece of white towelling
  for nappy (diaper)
Small pieces of white and pink
  felt for bib
Ribbon or lace for bib
Nappy (diaper) pin
Piece of red velvet
Piece of blue felt
50cm x 5cm (20in x 2in) red
  spotted material, cut on bias,
  for neckties
50cm (20in) narrow elastic

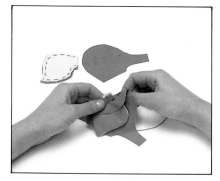

For each elephant the head should be made as follows. Cut the ear slits and pierce eye positions in the side head pieces. Sew the ears to the pink ear linings, leaving gap A-B open. Turn the ears the right way out and push the raw edge of the ears through the ear slits so that the pink lining faces forward towards the trunk. Sew across the slits.

With right sides together, sew the gusset to the side head from C to D. Repeat with the other side. Join seam E-F under the trunk. Flatten the end of the trunk so that the under trunk seam is in the centre of the top gusset. Sew across the end of the trunk.

Turn the head the right way out, poking out the trunk. Insert the safety eyes through the holes and secure with metal washers. Stuff the head, starting with the trunk. Mould the head into shape, pushing stuffing into the cheeks. Using a running stitch, sew around the raw edge of the neck, pull tight and finish off securely.

To make the bodies of the adult elephants, join the two body pieces between G and H, making sure the right sides are together. Repeat with other two body pieces, leaving a gap for stuffing. This will be the front body. Open out and place the front and back body pieces right sides together. Join across the top along seam J-G-J as shown.

Open out the body and match the arm piece to the body on either side between points K, J and K. Sew up the seams on both sides.

Fold the front and back body right sides together along the top seam. Sew the side seams from the tip of the arm to the foot, along M-K-L, on both sides of the body. Sew seam N-H-N between the legs.

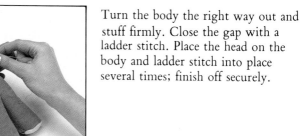

Open out the raw edges at the end of the arms and legs and, with right sides together, sew the pink foot pads into position.

Turn the body the right way out and stuff firmly. Close the gap with a ladder stitch. Place the head on the body and ladder stitch into place several times; finish off securely.

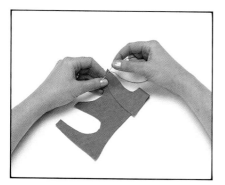

For the neckties, cut the fabric in half so each piece is about 25cm (10in) long. Tie each piece around the elephants' neck. Trim to fit as necessary. For the jackets, join the shoulder seams S-T on both sides. Turn the right way out but do not hem. Place on the elephants.

For the trousers, turn up a small hem along the bottom edges R-R on both pieces. Place the two halves right sides together and sew seam P-O on both sides. Join seam R-O-R between the trouser legs. Fold over the top of the trousers twice to make an elastic casing and sew in place, leaving a small gap. Insert the elastic and pull tight, adjusting to fit waist.

For the skirt, cut out a piece of velvet 14cm x 44cm (5½in x 17½in) and fold in half, right sides together. Sew along the short edge. Turn up a small hem and sew all around. Make an elastic casing using same method as for the trousers. Insert the narrow elastic and adjust to fit the waist of the mother elephant.

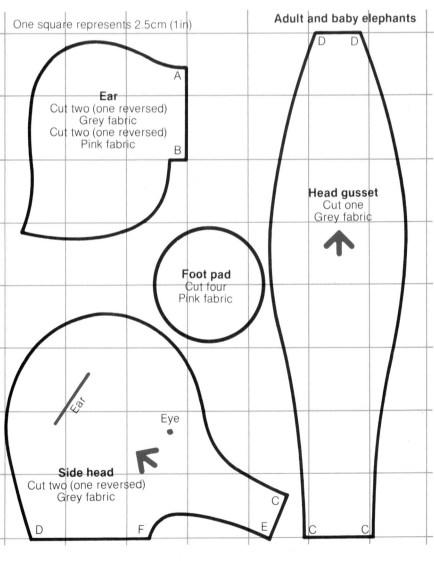

One square represents 2.5cm (1in)

Adult and baby elephants

D   D

Ear
Cut two (one reversed)
Grey fabric
Cut two (one reversed)
Pink fabric

A

B

Head gusset
Cut one
Grey fabric

Foot pad
Cut four
Pink fabric

Ear

Eye

Side head
Cut two (one reversed)
Grey fabric

D   F   E   C   C

C

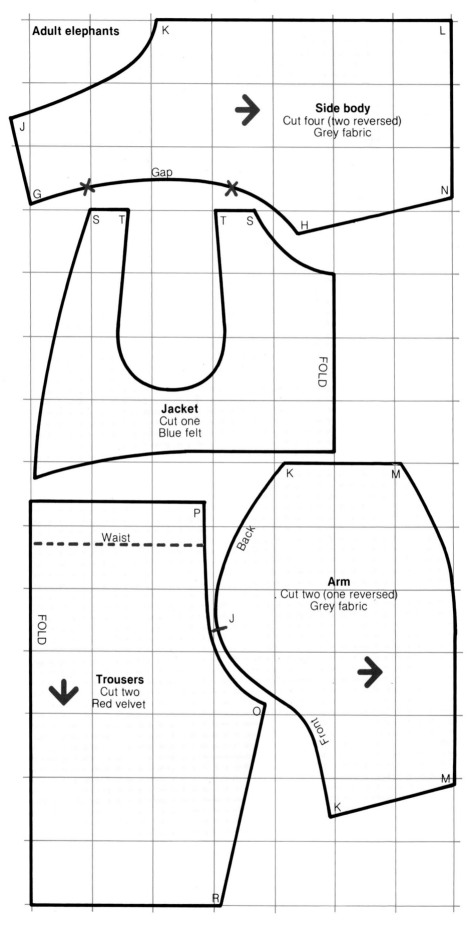

Adult elephants

K ⟶ L

Side body
Cut four (two reversed)
Grey fabric

J

G Gap N

Jacket
Cut one
Blue felt

FOLD

K M

Waist

P

Back

Arm
Cut two (one reversed)
Grey fabric

FOLD

J

Trousers
Cut two
Red velvet

O

Front

M

K

R

For the baby elephant, make the head according to the instructions on pages 102/3 (using pattern pieces on page 105). For the body, use the pattern on page 106. Join the two inside body pieces from A to B. Then join the side body pieces together by sewing from A to B, leaving a small gap for turning.

Join the inside body pieces to the side bodies by sewing seams A-C on either side, easing the fabric to fit. Then sew seam D-B-D around the base. Sew the foot pads into the leg openings on the body.

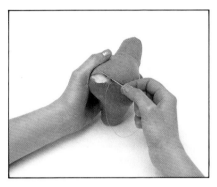

Turn the body the right way out and stuff. When satisfied with the shape, close the gap at the back using a ladder stitch.

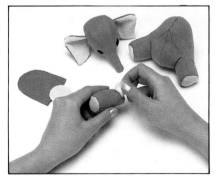

Sew around each pair of arms, leaving the bottom straight edge open. Open out the raw edges and sew in the foot pads. Snip a small slit at the top of each arm and turn the right way out. Stuff arms and oversew the gaps. Ladder stitch the head to the body and add arms on either side.

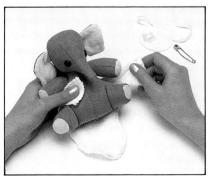

Turn in the raw edge all around the nappy (diaper) towelling and sew. Put on the baby elephant and secure with a pin. Sew a piece of ribbon or lace to the top edge of the bib and add a felt flower for decoration.

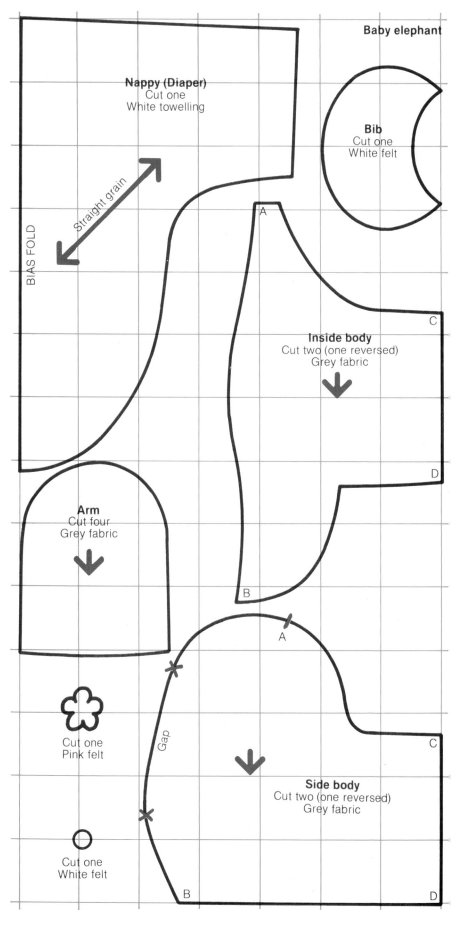

Baby elephant

Nappy (Diaper)
Cut one
White towelling

Straight grain

BIAS FOLD

Bib
Cut one
White felt

A

C

Inside body
Cut two (one reversed)
Grey fabric

D

Arm
Cut four
Grey fabric

B

A

Cut one
Pink felt

Gap

Cut one
White felt

Side body
Cut two (one reversed)
Grey fabric

C

B

D

MATERIALS

Black fur fabric
White fur fabric
Scraps of black felt
1 pair 13.5mm black safety
 eyes with metal washers
Black embroidery thread
Filling

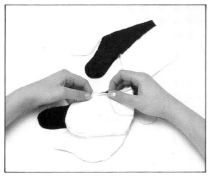

To join the three side body pieces together, first place the side head and middle body pieces right sides together and sew seam A-B. Then, with right sides together, match seam C-D of lower body piece and side middle body piece and sew. Repeat for other side.

Close the dart on the black upper inside body piece. Sew the black upper inside body to the white lower inside body along seam D-D. At the top neck edge, sew the upper inside body to the under chin piece along seam B-B.

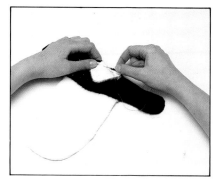

Sew the inside body to the side body between points G and F, matching points B and D, and easing the fabric to fit. Repeat on other side.

Sew the head gusset to the side head along seam E-A, making sure that point H matches. Repeat on other side. Close the seam E-G at the front of the head, then close the seam at the back of the panda from A to F.

Using sharp scissors, pierce tiny holes for the eyes at the position indicated. Then cut a slit down the centre of the white tummy. Turn the body the right way out through the slit, easing it out a little at a time. Be sure to poke out the ends of the arms.

Pierce a small hole in the eye patches. Insert the safety eyes through these holes, then through the holes in the head. Secure on the reverse side of the head with the washers. Fill the panda with stuffing, starting with the arms. Take care to shape the head and the nose. Close the gap in the tummy using a ladder stitch.

Fold one hind leg lengthwise and sew around it, leaving a gap for turning as indicated. Then turn the right way out and stuff lightly. Close the gap using a ladder stitch, then firmly ladder stitch the slightly fatter end of the leg to the side of the body using strong thread. Repeat for other leg.

Place two ear pieces right sides together and sew, leaving the straight edge open. Turn the right way out and oversew the raw edge. Repeat for other ear. Place the ears flat on the head and oversew into position. Then lift the ears upright and ladder stitch the front base of the ears down to the head to make them stand up.

With a long needle and black thread, tack the eye patches down to the head at both the top and the bottom. Using long straight stitches, embroider a nose and mouth on the panda. Then, if desired, use white thread to stitch claws on each paw.

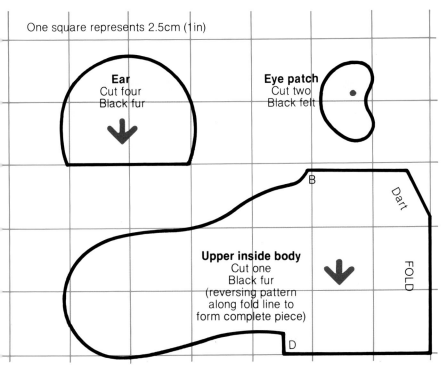

One square represents 2.5cm (1in)

Ear
Cut four
Black fur

Eye patch
Cut two
Black felt

B

Dart

FOLD

Upper inside body
Cut one
Black fur
(reversing pattern
along fold line to
form complete piece)

D

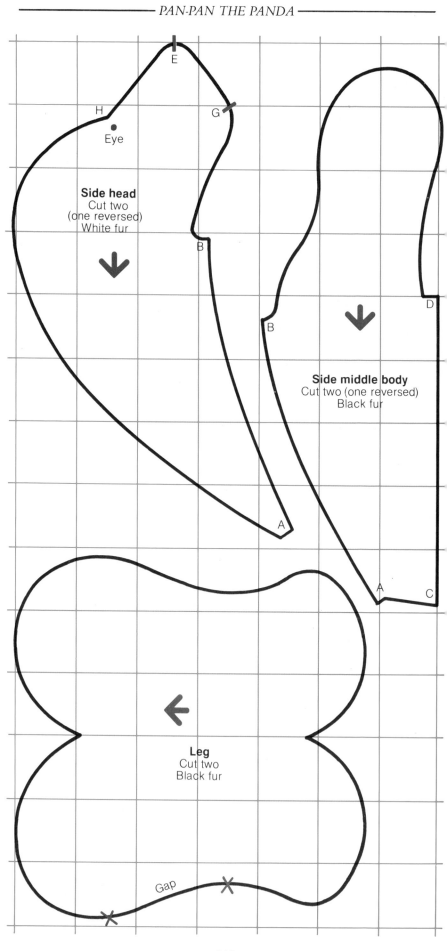

E

H
• Eye

Side head
Cut two
(one reversed)
White fur

G

B

B

D

Side middle body
Cut two (one reversed)
Black fur

A

A   C

Leg
Cut two
Black fur

Gap

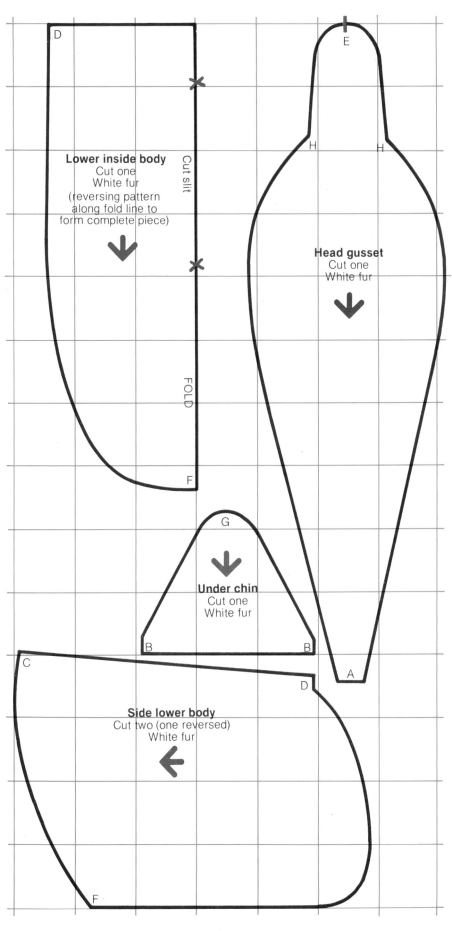

D

Lower inside body
Cut one
White fur
(reversing pattern
along fold line to
form complete piece)

Cut slit

X

X

FOLD

F

E

H   H

Head gusset
Cut one
White fur

G

Under chin
Cut one
White fur

B   B

C

D

A

Side lower body
Cut two (one reversed)
White fur

F

MATERIALS

Dark brown fur fabric
Beige fur fabric
Yellow felt for banana
White felt for banana
1 pair 13.5mm brown safety
    eyes with metal washers
Thick black embroidery thread
Filling

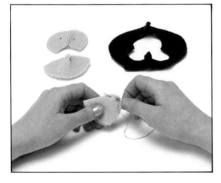

With right sides together, sew the two side head pieces together from A to B and from C to D. Then sew the darts on the upper face piece and the muzzle pieces.

Join the upper face to one of the muzzle pieces together from E to E making sure the notches and the dart seams match. Then sew the two muzzle pieces together from E to E along the dart-free edges.

With right sides together, join the face to the side head pieces, carefully matching the points all the way around. Join the two back head pieces together by sewing seam A-G.

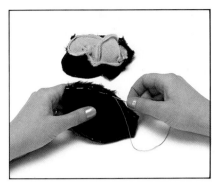

Open out the back head and place it against the completed front head with the right sides together. Sew all the way around, leaving the neck edge open.

Pierce tiny holes for the eyes in the position indicated on the pattern. Turn the head the right way out. Insert the safety eyes through the holes and secure on the reverse with the washers.

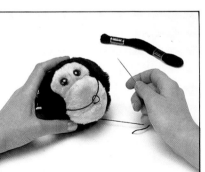

Fill the head with stuffing, easing it gently into shape. Gather the raw neck edge with a running stitch and fasten off securely. Using thick black embroidery thread and a long needle, stitch a long smile across the monkey's face with a single stitch on the seam line. Anchor the smile down with a second stitch across the centre as shown.

Sew the ears together in pairs, leaving the straight edge open. Turn the ears and form a pleat at the raw edge, oversewing into position as shown. Attach the ears by oversewing them flat onto the head, then lifting them upright and ladder stitching the front base of the ears down to the head to make them stand up. Place head to one side.

Sew the dart on the side body pieces. On one pair of legs and arms, mark out a circle as shown on the pattern. Lay the side body pieces right side up. Place the arms and leg pieces onto the body with the wrong side up. The legs should be pointing straight out, but the arms can be either up or down. Pin the limbs to the body in the centre of the circles and stitch carefully around the circles.

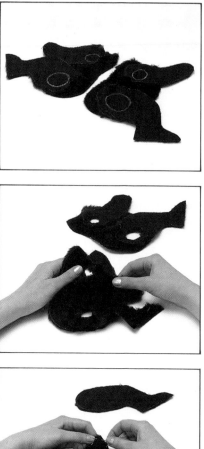

With a pair of sharp pointed scissors, cut out the centre of the circles about 5mm (¼in) from the stitching line. Push one arm right through the hole so that the wrong sides of the fabric are facing each other. Repeat with the other arm and the legs.

Take the remaining limb pieces and pair them up with each arm and leg attached to the body. Sew all the way around the arms, not leaving a gap. For the legs, sew around the curved edges, but leave the straight edge open for the foot pads.

Ease the foot pads into the bottom of the legs, making sure that the right sides are together and the narrow end is at the heel. Sew the foot pads into place, easing the fabric gently to fit if necessary.

Turn the limbs the right way out, back through the holes in the side body. Then join the two sides together all the way around, keeping the legs tucked in and leaving the neck edge J-K open. Turn the body through the neck opening.

Fill the arms and legs, then the body cavity. Close the gap at the neck and ladder stitch the head to the body, adjusting the position of the head to create a cheeky pose. Fold the tail in half lengthwise. Sew along the long curved edge, leaving the top straight edge open. Turn the tail the right way out and tuck the raw edge under. Ladder stitch the tail to the body.

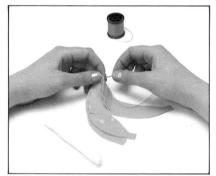

To make the banana, join the three white felt pieces together, leaving a small gap for turning. Turn and stuff firmly, then close the gap. Sew the three yellow outside skin pieces together halfway along the length. Turn the right way out and push the white banana down into the skin as far as it will go.

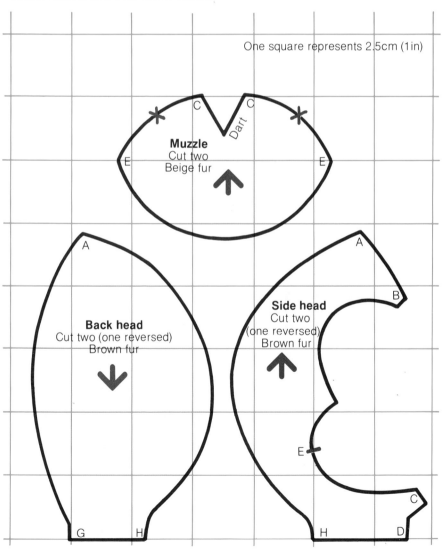

One square represents 2.5cm (1in)

Muzzle
Cut two
Beige fur

Back head
Cut two (one reversed)
Brown fur

Side head
Cut two
(one reversed)
Brown fur

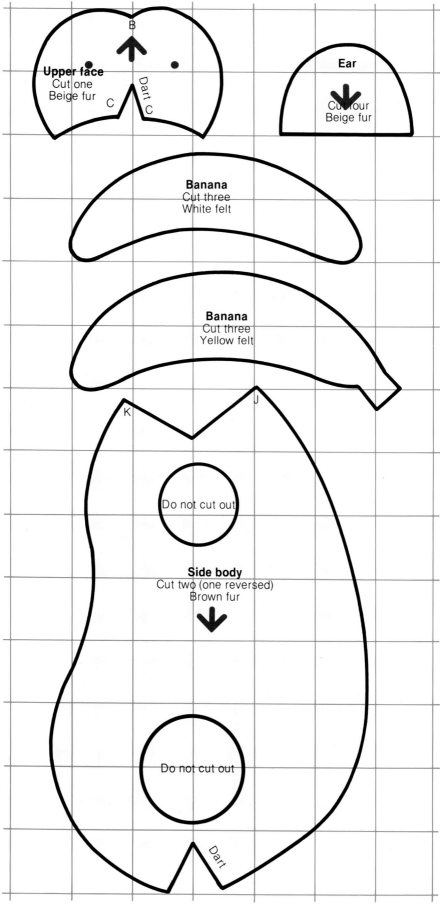

Upper face
Cut one
Beige fur

B

Dart C

C

Ear
Cut four
Beige fur

Banana
Cut three
White felt

Banana
Cut three
Yellow felt

K

J

Do not cut out

Side body
Cut two (one reversed)
Brown fur

Do not cut out

Dart

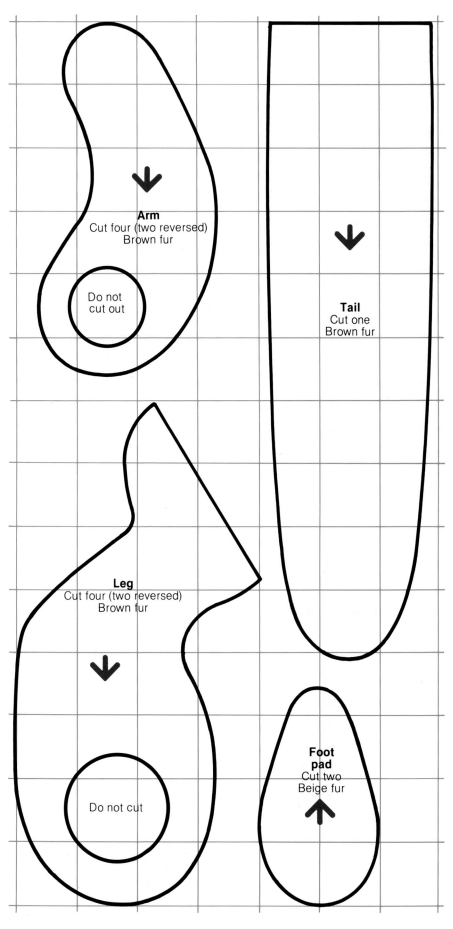

Arm
Cut four (two reversed)
Brown fur

Do not
cut out

Tail
Cut one
Brown fur

Leg
Cut four (two reversed)
Brown fur

Do not cut

**Foot
pad**
Cut two
Beige fur

MATERIALS

30cm (12in) white fur fabric
1 pair 13.5mm black safety
    eyes with metal washers
1 small plastic nose
Black embroidery thread
Filling

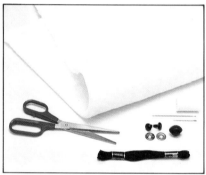

Pierce a tiny hole at the eye position and cut a slit for the ears on each side body piece, then place to one side. Join both pieces of the inside body by sewing seam A-B, leaving a gap for turning and filling. Open out the inside body. Sew the under chin piece to the inside body along seam C-A-C.

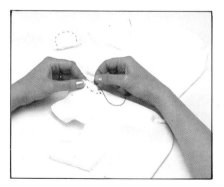

Sew up the darts at the rear of the side body pieces. Sew both halves of ears together, leaving the straight edge open. Turn the right way out and make a small tuck at the raw edge of the ear on both sides to curve the ear slightly inwards and oversew into place. Push the straight edge through the slit in the side body and sew the ears into position through all layers of fabric.

Join the head gusset piece to the side of the head on the side body piece by sewing seam J-K. Repeat on other side. Then sew up seam J-D at the front of the head.

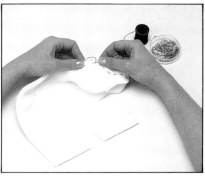

Sew the inside body to the side body, starting at seam D-E. Then sew seam F-G and finally seam H-B. Repeat on other side.

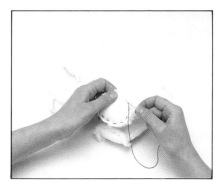

Fold the tail in half lengthwise. Sew along the curved edge, leaving the top open. Turn the tail, poking out the tip carefully. Sew seam K-B on the back of the bear, sewing in the tail at the same time where the two darts meet. Open out and stretch the bottoms of the feet and sew in the foot pads.

Turn the bear the right way out. Insert the safety eyes through the holes made earlier and secure on the reverse with metal washers. Poke a tiny hole at the very end of the snout and secure the plastic nose in the same way.

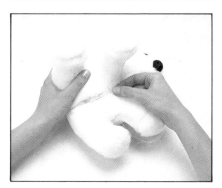

Fill the bear with stuffing, starting at the feet. Flatten the feet slightly as the filling is added. Mould the head shape by pushing more filling into the cheeks. When satisfied with the general shape of the bear, close the gap in the tummy using a ladder stitch.

With black embroidery thread, stitch through the feet four times on each paw to form claws. Using the same thread, embroider a smile on the bear's face, referring to the relevant part of the instructions on page 17. Finish off the mouth on either side with a small stitch at right angles to the main stitch.

Finally, taking a long needle and white thread, pull the eyes slightly together by passing the threaded needle from corner to corner of the opposite eyes, through the head. Fasten off securely.

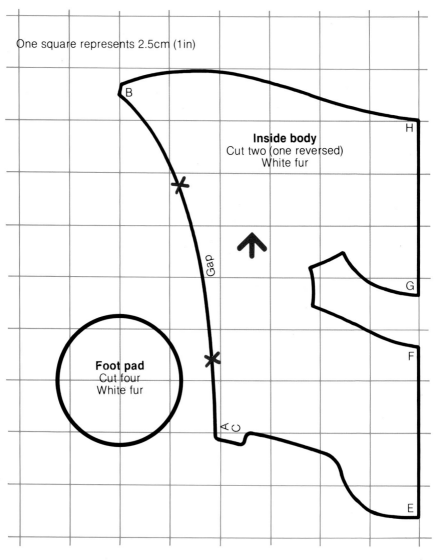

One square represents 2.5cm (1in)

B

H

Inside body
Cut two (one reversed)
White fur

Gap

G

Foot pad
Cut four
White fur

F

A
C

E

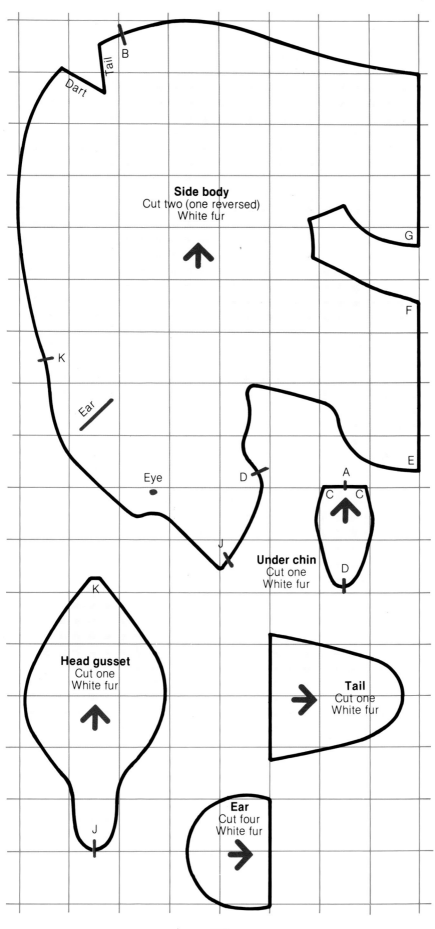

Side body
Cut two (one reversed)
White fur

Under chin
Cut one
White fur

Head gusset
Cut one
White fur

Tail
Cut one
White fur

Ear
Cut four
White fur

MATERIALS

30cm (12in) gold fur fabric
Scrap of long gold fur fabric
1 pair 15mm brown safety
    eyes with metal washers
Thick black embroidery thread
Filling

On both side body pieces, close the darts at the rear and the neck. Pierce tiny holes at the eye position and cut slits for ears. Sew around each pair of ears, leaving the straight edge open. Turn the ears and make a small tuck at the base. Oversew into place. Push the raw edges into the slits made earlier and sew into position through all layers of fur.

To join the chin piece to the head gusset, place them right sides together and sew along seam A-B. Then, also with right sides together, sew the chin piece to the under body along seam C-D.

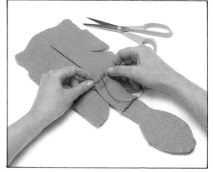

Sew the gussets to the side body between points E and G, ensuring that points F, A/B and the notches match. Then sew seam H-J and K-L. Repeat on other side.

Open out the raw edges of the feet and stretch them gently. With right sides together, place the foot pads around the raw edges of the feet and sew them into place.

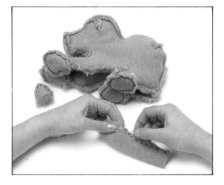

Take the tail tuft pieces and, with right sides together, sew along the curved edges. Trim close to the edge and turn. Fold the tail piece lengthwise and sew along the long edge. Poke the tuft into the tail and, with the raw edges level, sew across the top. Turn the tail the right way out. Sew seam E-L along the lion's back, sewing the tail into place at the same time.

Turn the lion the right way out. Insert the eyes through the holes made earlier and secure on the reverse with metal washers. Fill the lion with stuffing, pushing it gently into the cheeks to give them a rounded shape. Close the slit on the inside body using a ladder stitch.

Using thick black thread, embroider a nose on the lion with several straight stitches, then add a mouth, referring to the instructions on page 17. Using the same thread double thickness, stitch through the feet four times on each paw to form claws.

One square represents 2.5cm (1in)

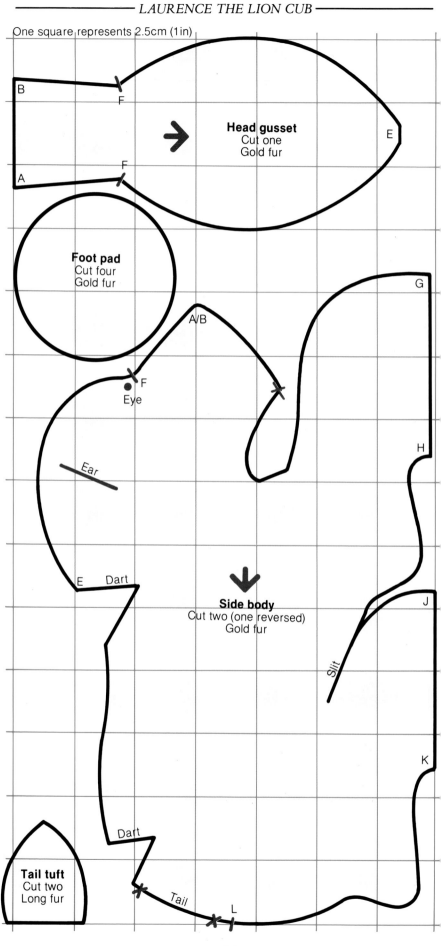

Head gusset
Cut one
Gold fur

Foot pad
Cut four
Gold fur

Side body
Cut two (one reversed)
Gold fur

Tail tuft
Cut two
Long fur

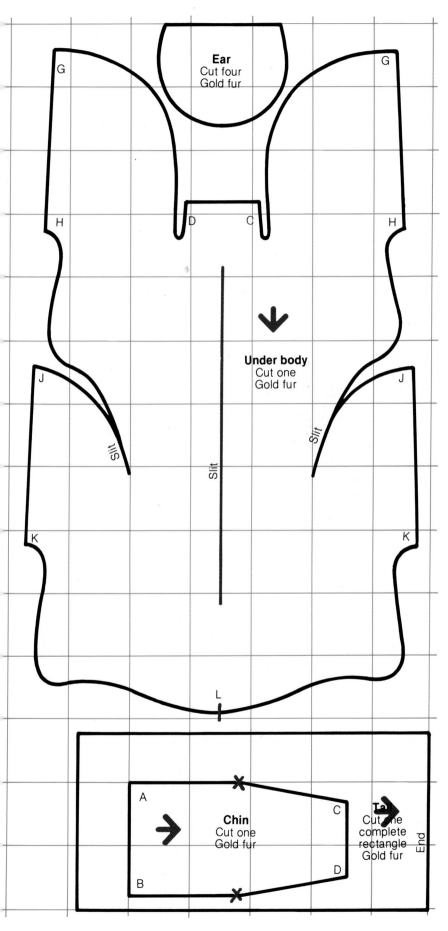

Ear
Cut four
Gold fur

G

G

H

H

Under body
Cut one
Gold fur

J

J

Slit

Slit

Slit

K

K

L

A

C

Chin
Cut one
Gold fur

B

D

Tail
Cut one
complete
rectangle
Gold fur

End